CH00894541

high vitality cooking

high vitality cooking

OVER 70 RECIPES TO IMPROVE HEALTH, FITNESS AND ENERGY

MAGGIE PANNELL

LORENZ BOOKS

This edition is published by Lorenz Books
Lorenz Books is an imprint of Anness Publishing Ltd
Hermes House, 88–89 Blackfriars Road, London SE1 8HA
tel. 020 7401 2077; fax 020 7633 9499
www.lorenzbooks.com; info@anness.com

This edition distributed in the UK by Aurum Press Ltd, 25 Bedford Avenue,
London WC1B 3AT; tel. 020 7637 3225; fax 020 7580 2469
This edition distributed in the USA and Canada by National Book Network, 4720 Boston Way,
Lanham, MD 20706; tel. 301 459 3366; fax 301 459 1705; www.nbnbooks.com
This edition distributed in Australia by Pan Macmillan Australia,
Level 18, St Martins Tower, 31 Market St, Sydney, NSW 2000;
tel. 1300 135 113; fax 1300 135 103; customer.service@macmillan.com.au
This edition distributed in New Zealand by David Bateman Ltd,
30 Tarndale Grove, Off Bush Road, Albany, Auckland; tel. (09) 415 7664; fax (09) 415 8892

A CIP catalogue record for this book is available from the British Library

Publisher: Joanna Lorenz
Senior Cookery Editor: Linda Fraser
Cookery Editor: Maggie Mayhew
Designer: Siân Keogh
Photography: Karl Adamson
Food for Photography: Katherine Hawkins
Stylist: Marion McLornan
Illustrator: Madeleine David
Previously published as part of the Creative Cooking Library

Printed and bound in China

1 3 5 7 9 10 8 6 4 2

Notes
For all recipes, quantities are given in both metric and imperial measures and, where appropriate, measures are also given in standard cups and spoons. Follow one set, but not a mixture because they are not interchangeable.

Standard spoon and cup measurements are level.
1tsp = 5ml, 1tbsp = 15ml, 1 cup = 250ml/8floz

Australian standard tablespoons are 20ml. Australian readers should use 3tsp in place of 1 tbsp for measuring small quantities of gelatine, cornflour, salt etc.

Medium eggs should be used unless otherwise stated.

Contents

INTRODUCTION

Do you often feel tired and sluggish? Have you lost that get-up-and-go feeling? How often have you wished you could pack more into your day if only you had the energy? Life is frequently physically and mentally demanding, but it can also be a lot of fun and very rewarding. Naturally, there will always be difficult times and stressful situations that can leave you feeling drained, weary and lethargic, but the good news is that you can have control over how active and alert you feel. Simply by putting the right fuel into your body, you will be able to cope much better with whatever life throws at you. Eat for vitality and you'll discover renewed zest for life, lots more stamina and a more positive outlook.

HOW TO ACHIEVE HIGH ENERGY

It is essential to choose the right balance of foods. Today we are spoilt for choice in the supermarket. The shelves are crammed with all kinds of exciting foreign foods, convenience foods and new products. The choice is so enormous that shopping can be quite bewildering!

Also, a great many foods just look so appealing that it's all too easy to be tempted by the photograph on the packaging and to make compulsive purchases rather than make sensible selections based on a sound and informed knowledge of nutrition.

Fortunately, despite some of the unhealthy temptations, there is also a fabulous selection of fresh convenience foods on offer, such as ready-prepared packs of salads and vegetables for stir-frying, which make preparing fresh and wholesome meals quick and easy. Look out for healthy eating symbols, such as "high fibre" or "low fat" on food products, although it is wise to read the nutrition panel too, as such claims can often mask other factors such as a high sugar content.

All food provides nutrients and energy, which is measured in kilocalories or kilojoules. In Western society, there is little likelihood of consuming too few calories (except in cases of eating disorders, such as anorexia nervosa) but there is a real risk of going short on essential nutrients, or at least of not getting the best from the food we eat. This is because certain foods provide much better nutrient value than others. Foods which are lacking in good nutrient value are often said to provide "empty" calories because they contribute little else, other than calories, and can therefore be regarded as unnecessary foods (see Foods to Avoid, page 7).

For optimum nutritional and therefore vitality value, choose a fresh wholefood diet containing a wide variety of different foods. This will ensure a good intake of nutrients, particularly the vitamins and minerals essential for helping to generate a good, steady release of energy.

Left: Combine eating a balanced diet with regular exercise.

THE ESSENTIAL ENERGISERS

Although it's very easy to recommend following a balanced diet, in reality diets and eating habits are frequently far from ideal. We rush from appointment to appointment, eat on the run, miss meals, dine out in restaurants or fast-food outlets and seldom stop to think about what we really should be eating. Also, because every individual is different, needs vary, so it is worth considering more closely which nutrients are particularly important in combating fatigue.

The mineral iron is essential for the formation of red blood cells and therefore the oxygen-carrying capacity of the blood. Anaemia due to iron deficiency is a common problem in rapidly growing teenagers, women with heavy periods, pregnant women (due to the extra requirement needed for a growing baby) and vegetarians who cut out meat without including other good vegetarian sources of iron. Fish helps provide iron.

Zinc deficiency can also contribute to fatigue and because red meat is the main source from which it is readily absorbed, vegetarians can be at risk if they do not include other sources, like eggs, wholegrain cereals, dried fruit, corn on the cob and sesame seeds.

The B-group vitamins are crucial for their role in helping to release energy from food. Vitamin B12 also helps protect against anaemia. B-group vitamins are sensitive to heat and are water-soluble, so nutrient-friendly cooking methods should be followed (see Cooking for Vitality, page 9).

Vitamin C helps the body to absorb iron from vegetable sources. So, for example, drinking fresh orange or tomato juice with a vegetarian meal will increase the uptake of iron. All fruit and vegetables are sources of vitamin C. Like the B-group vitamins, vitamin C is also unstable and it is easily destroyed, so it pays to be a careful cook.

Vitamin E also improves the oxygen-carrying capacity of the blood and helps to increase stamina. Good sources of this vitamin include vegetable oils, wheatgerm, eggs, wholemeal bread and nuts.

The key to maximum energy is keeping the blood-sugar level constant. The best foods for doing this are complex, unrefined carbohydrates – wholegrain cereals, pulses, starchy fruit and vegetables – because they are digested more slowly and release a steady stream of sugar into the blood. These foods are also a good source of dietary fibre, which is essential for a healthy digestive system.

It is important to eat regular meals and not to skip breakfast. The body needs fuel in the morning after its long overnight break. It is also true that those who fail to eat something sustaining for breakfast are much more likely to snack on whatever is quickest and closest to hand mid-morning, which is unlikely to be a good nutritional choice.

Above: It's important to make time for breakfast and to eat regular meals throughout the day.

Foods to Avoid

The aim should be to cut down on saturated fats, refined carbohydrates and highly processed foods as these tend to be high in the fats and sugars that pile on unnecessary calories and sap your energy. The list includes most cakes, sweets, chocolates, biscuits, fried foods, rich, creamy sauces and pastries. Sugary carbohydrates may give an instant lift, as they are digested quickly and release sugar rapidly into the bloodstream, but the body compensates by releasing a surge of insulin which pulls the blood-sugar level down low again, resulting in a sudden drop of energy. Such fluctuations cause tiredness rather than a steady prolonged feeling of well-being. Stimulants, like coffee, tea and alcohol have a similar effect. The caffeine and theobromines in coffee and tea give you a temporary lift, because like alcohol, they cause a rapid release of sugar into the bloodstream, but the effect is short-lived.

These stimulants are also diuretics, so many of the water-soluble vitamins B and C are lost. The tannin in tea inhibits the absorption of iron, and too much caffeine causes insomnia.

Alcohol also depletes stores of vitamins B and C which are needed to detoxify the body. Alcohol and cigarettes both impair the absorption of B vitamins and increase the need for vitamin C.

Ingredients for Vitality

Vitality Drinks

Good choices for vitality drinks are decaffeinated coffee, herbal teas or weak Ceylon and China teas, mineral water and fresh fruit juices.

Foods for Vitality

Wholegrain Cereals: A good source of vegetable protein, iron, B vitamins and vitamin E, wholegrain cereals (brown rice, wholewheat bread and pasta, oats, millet, buckwheat, pot barley and bulgur wheat) provide much more fibre than refined cereals. Eat plenty of bread, including the many different international varieties, such as Indian naan bread and chapatis, Italian ciabatta (made with olive oil), or Scandinavian and German rye breads. Aim to have about six slices of bread a day – without butter.

Pulses: These are good sources of protein, starch carbohydrates, fibre, B vitamins and minerals. If you haven't got time to soak dried pulses, canned varieties are just as good. Add them to soups, stews and salads, and experiment with dishes based on beans, lentils and tofu (soya bean curd).

Fruit and Vegetables: Vitamin C is found almost exclusively in fruit and vegetables and because this vitamin cannot be stored by the body, levels need to be topped up continually.

Above: Include a variety of breads, such as ciabatta and German rye bread.

Above: A variety of fresh fruit is important for maintaining vitamin C levels.

Green vegetables, red peppers, citrus fruits, tomatoes, strawberries, kiwi fruit, cranberries and blackcurrants are particularly good sources. Potatoes, too, are an important source of vitamin C, simply because they are eaten so often and in such quantity. They are also a very versatile food source.

Beta-carotene (which the body converts to vitamin A) and vitamin E are also present in many fruits and vegetables. Several green vegetables, such as broccoli, Brussels sprouts, cabbage, kale and spinach, are excellent sources of beta-carotene as is brightly-coloured yellow, red and orange produce, such as carrots, apricots, mangoes, peaches and melon. Some good sources of vitamin E include blackberries, asparagus, avocados, broccoli, sweet potatoes, spinach, tomatoes, parsley and watercress.

Fruit and vegetables are also extremely rich in fibre, particularly when eaten with the skin on. Aim to eat at least five portions of fresh fruit and vegetables a day. Use frozen produce when fresh is not available – it is perfectly acceptable from a nutritional point of view.

Dried Fruits: These are an excellent source of minerals, particularly iron, calcium and potassium. Eat raw or cooked for a healthy snack.

Fish: All fish is rich in protein, B vitamins and minerals. White fish is very low in fat. Oily fish, such as sardines, mackerel, herring, tuna, trout and salmon, also provide vitamins A and D and Omega 3 fatty acids, which are believed to be beneficial in helping to prevent coronary heart disease.

Eggs: Virtually a complete food, eggs provide protein, iron, zinc and vitamins A, B-group and E.

Poultry: A good source of quality protein, B vitamins and some iron, poultry is also low in fat, particularly if the skin is removed.

Meat and Game: Although the general health advice is to moderate your intake of red meat, thus reducing the amount of saturated fat in your diet, red meat is still the best source of readily absorbed iron, zinc and B vitamins. Meat today is much leaner than it used to be, and it fits the profile for a healthy diet if it is cooked with low-fat cooking methods.

Fats and Oils: Stick to low-fat products like yogurt and skimmed or semi-skimmed milk, not just for a healthier, general reduction in fat intake, but also because fats require more oxygen for their metabolism and are therefore a constant drain on the body's resources.

A moderate intake of fats and oils is

Above: Many fresh vegetables also help provide beta-carotene and all are rich in fibre.

Above: Eat a variety of oily and white fish, such as tuna, plaice, salmon, and trout.

essential. They provide vitamins A and D, and dairy products are the best source of calcium. Switch to oils high in unsaturates, like sunflower, soya, grapeseed, corn and olive oil – the mainstay of the Mediterranean diet – and reserve butter for special occasions when flavour really counts.

Garlic: This is reputed to have all kinds of health benefits, including helping to increase overall strength and vitality and reducing lethargy. Use it fresh or cooked, in salads, dressings and main dishes.

Nuts and Seeds: Nuts are an excellent source of protein, particularly for vegetarians. They are rich in B-group and E vitamins and provide many minerals, especially iron, zinc and potassium. Pumpkin, sunflower and sesame seeds are also rich in vitamin E and calcium. However, nuts and seeds have a high oil content (albeit mainly unsaturated) so watch the calories.

COOKING FOR VITALITY

Eat as much raw food as possible. Vitamins B and C are particularly unstable and are easily destroyed by heat, so include plenty of salads in your diet. Use really fresh produce, and prepare just before eating. Keep a well-stocked fruit bowl for between-meal nibbles.

Cook vegetables in the minimum amount of water or steam them. Reserve any cooking water to add to soups, stews and sauces.

Trim all visible fat from meat and remove skin from poultry. If the skin is required to keep the flesh succulent, remove after cooking.

Choose low-fat cooking methods, such as grilling, stir-frying, steaming, poaching, casseroling, baking and microwaving, wherever possible.

Use the minimum amount of oil for cooking and choose a type that is low in saturated fats, like olive oil or sunflower oil.

Substitute low-fat yogurt, fromage frais or half-fat crème fraîche for cream and use reduced-fat cheeses. Parmesan and other strong-tasting cheeses are useful because you only need to use a little for a lot of flavour.

Even if you are not a vegetarian, aim to have a vegetarian meal once or twice a week. Alternatively, use less meat in dishes and make up the quantity with pulses and vegetables.

THE IMPORTANCE OF EXERCISE

Any form of aerobic exercise increases your intake of oxygen and improves your circulation, making the heart and all the muscles work more efficiently.

Above: Nuts and seeds not only provide essential B vitamins, minerals and protein, they also make a tasty treat.

Above: Garlic is very beneficial in helping to maintain good health.

Exercise creates a feeling of well-being and is wonderful for relieving stress and fatigue. It doesn't particularly matter how you choose to exercise, but pick something you enjoy, do it on a regular basis and don't over-exert yourself.

BONUS HEALTH BENEFITS

Following a high vitality diet will automatically help you to control a desirable weight. Kilocalories and kilojoule counts have been included on the recipes for reference, but if you choose the right balance of foods, and take regular exercise, your weight should reach a healthy level without dieting. This will help to protect you against common health risks, such as coronary heart disease, certain cancers, high blood pressure, strokes, diabetes and arthritis, all of which can be attributed to an unhealthy diet.

Reducing fat intake is of particular importance. Aim to have a total fat intake of no more than 30% of your daily kilocalories. That should work out at between 70g and 90g a day.

Eat plenty of vitamin- and mineral-rich foods and see how your skin becomes clearer and your hair shinier. In fact, you can look forward to looking and feeling wonderful.

Breakfasts and Brunches

A good start in the morning is essential if you want to feel vital and alert the whole day through. Don't make the excuse of not having enough time. All the ideas here are quick to prepare and eat, yet sustaining and full of nutritional value to keep your energy levels well topped up and hunger at bay. Skip breakfast, and you're likely to succumb to far less nutritious mid-morning snacks.

Melon, Pineapple and Grape Cocktail

A light fresh fruit salad, with no added sugar, makes a refreshing start to the day, and can easily be prepared the night before.

Ingredients

Serves 4

½ melon
225g/8oz fresh pineapple, or 227g/8oz can pineapple chunks in own juice
225g/8oz seedless white grapes, halved
120ml/4fl oz/½ cup white grape juice
fresh mint leaves, to decorate (optional)

1 Remove the seeds from the melon half and use a melon baller to scoop out even-size balls.

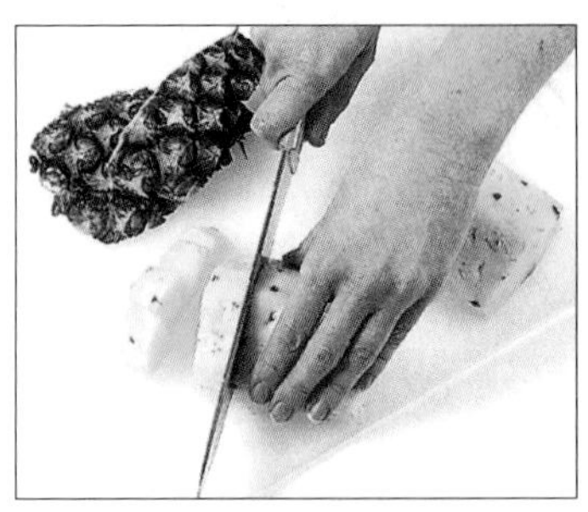

2 Using a sharp knife, cut the skin from the pineapple and discard. Cut the fruit into bite-size chunks.

3 Combine all the fruits in a glass serving dish and pour over the juice. If you are using canned pineapple, measure the drained juice and make it up to the required quantity with grape juice.

4 If not serving immediately, cover and chill. Serve decorated with mint leaves, if liked.

Nutritional Notes
Per Portion

Energy	95Kcals/395KJ
Fat	0.5g
Saturated Fat	0
Cholesterol	0

Three Fruit Compôtes

INGREDIENTS

Each Compôte Serves 1

Orange and Prune Compôte
1 juicy orange, peeled
50g/2oz/⅓ cup ready-to-eat prunes
75ml/5 tbsp orange juice

Pear and Kiwi Fruit Compôte
1 ripe eating pear, cored
1 kiwi fruit
60ml/4 tbsp apple or pineapple juice

Grapefruit and Strawberry Compôte
1 ruby grapefruit, peeled
115g/4oz strawberries
60ml/4 tbsp orange juice

To serve
yogurt and toasted hazelnuts

1 For the orange and prune compôte, segment the orange and place in a bowl with the prunes.

2 For the pear and kiwi fruit compôte, slice the pear. Peel and cut the kiwi fruit into wedges.

3 For the grapefruit and strawberry compôte, segment the grapefruit and halve the strawberries.

4 Place your selected fruits together in a bowl and pour over the juice. Choose "fresh-pressed" juices rather than those made from concentrates. Or, squeeze your own juice using a blender or food processor.

5 Serve the chosen compôte topped with a spoonful of low-fat natural yogurt together with a sprinkling of chopped toasted hazelnuts.

NUTRITIONAL NOTES

Per Portion (without topping)

Orange and Prune Compôte	
Energy	155Kcals/650KJ
Fat	0.5g

Pear and Kiwi Fruit Compôte	
Energy	100Kcals/405KJ
Fat	0.5g

Grapefruit and Strawberry Compôte	
Energy	110Kcals/465KJ
Fat	0.5g

Neither saturated fat nor cholesterol is present in any of the compôtes.

Date, Banana and Walnut Yogurt

Dates and bananas give a high fibre boost to this breakfast. Both fruits are also high in natural sugars.

INGREDIENTS

Serves 4

115g/4oz/⅔ cup dried dates, stoned and chopped
300ml/½ pint/1¼ cups low-fat natural yogurt
2 bananas
50g/2oz/½ cup chopped walnuts

COOK'S TIP

Use standard dried dates and not those which have been sugar-rolled. Bananas are probably the best and most convenient instant-energy food there is. If you haven't got time for breakfast, just unzip a banana!

1 Stir the dates into the yogurt in a mixing bowl. Cover and leave overnight in the fridge, to allow the fruit to soften.

2 Peel, then slice the bananas into the yogurt mixture. Spoon into dishes and top with the walnuts.

NUTRITIONAL NOTES

Per Portion

Energy	225Kcals/1060KJ
Fat	9.5g
Saturated Fat	1.5g
Cholesterol	3mg

Mixed Berry Yogurt Shake

Whizz this in a blender or food processor for a quick, low-fat and high vitality breakfast in a glass. Rosewater adds an exotic touch. You could also experiment with other fruits to create your own flavour shake, such as banana with vanilla essence, or apricot with a few drops of almond essence.

INGREDIENTS

Serves 2

250ml/8fl oz/1 cup semi-skimmed milk, chilled
250ml/8fl oz/1 cup low-fat natural yogurt
115g/4oz mixed summer fruits
5ml/1 tsp rosewater
a little honey, to taste

1 Blend the milk, yogurt, fruits and rosewater in a food processor.

NUTRITIONAL NOTES

Per Portion

Energy	125Kcals/520KJ
Fat	3.5g
Saturated Fat	2g
Cholesterol	14mg

2 Add honey to taste if necessary, depending on the sweetness of the fruits. Pour into two glasses.

COOK'S TIP

Any combination of soft red fruits can be used, such as strawberries, raspberries, bilberries, blackberries, morello cherries and/or redcurrants.

Cheese and Banana Toasties

Wholemeal toast topped with reduced-fat soft cheese and sliced banana makes the perfect high-fibre breakfast and is especially delicious when drizzled with honey and grilled. It's easy to make, and provides a delicious start to any day.

Ingredients

Serves 4

4 thick slices of wholemeal bread
115g/4oz/½ cup reduced-fat soft cheese
1.5ml/¼ tsp cardamom seeds, crushed (optional)
4 small bananas, peeled
20ml/4 tsp clear honey

1 Place the bread on a rack in a grill pan and toast on one side only.

2 Turn the bread over, and spread the untoasted side of each slice with soft cheese. Sprinkle over the crushed cardamom seeds, if using.

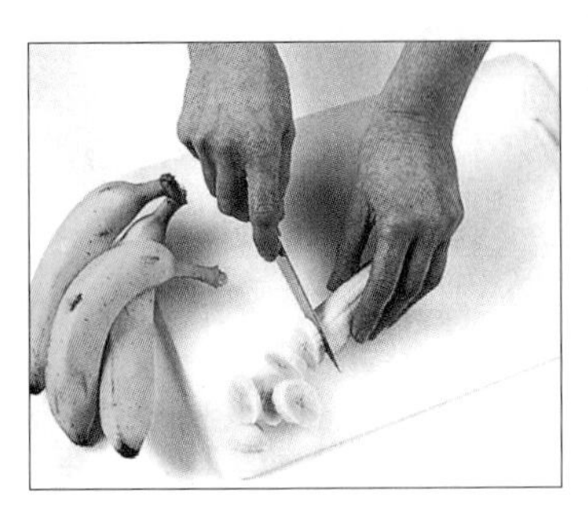

3 Slice the bananas and arrange the slices on top of the cheese. Then drizzle each slice with 5ml/1 tsp of the clear honey. Slide the pan back under the moderately hot grill and leave for a few minutes until bubbling. Serve immediately.

Cook's Tip

For a delicious variation, use fruited, sesame seed or caraway seed wholemeal bread. Omit the cardamom seeds and sprinkle ground cinnamon on the bananas before adding the honey.

Nutritional Notes

Per Portion

Energy	240Kcals/1005KJ
Fat	4.5g
Saturated Fat	2g
Cholesterol	4mg

Mixed Pepper Pipérade

Ingredients

Serves 4

30ml/2 tbsp olive oil
1 onion, chopped
1 red pepper
1 green pepper
4 tomatoes, peeled and chopped
1 garlic clove, crushed
4 size 2 eggs, beaten with 15ml/1 tbsp water
ground black pepper
4 large, thick slices of wholemeal toast, to serve

1 Heat the oil in a large frying pan and sauté the onion gently until it becomes softened.

2 Remove the seeds from the red and green peppers and slice them thinly. Stir the pepper slices into the onion and cook together gently for 5 minutes. Add the tomatoes and garlic, season with black pepper, and cook for a further 5 minutes.

3 Pour the egg mixture over the vegetables in the frying pan and cook for 2–3 minutes, stirring now and then, until the pipérade has thickened to the consistency of lightly scrambled eggs. Serve immediately with warm wholemeal toast.

Cook's Tip

Choose eggs that have been date-stamped for freshness. Do not stir the pipérade too much or the eggs may become rubbery.

Nutritional Notes

Per Portion

Energy	310Kcals/1300KJ
Fat	14.5g
Saturated Fat	3g
Cholesterol	231mg

Fruity Sesame Porridge

Porridge made with skimmed milk makes a wonderfully nourishing breakfast. Dried fruit and toasted sesame seeds make it even better, providing useful amounts of iron and magnesium.

Ingredients

Serves 2

50g/2oz/½ cup porridge oats
475ml/16fl oz/2 cups skimmed milk
75g/3oz/½ cup ready-to-eat dried fruit salad, chopped
30ml/2 tbsp sesame seeds, toasted

1 Put the oats, milk and chopped dried fruit in a non-stick saucepan.

Cook's Tip

If you use so-called "old-fashioned" or "original" oats, the porridge will be quite thick and coarse textured. You could also use "jumbo" oats. If you prefer a smoother porridge, try ordinary rolled oats (sometimes called oatflakes).

2 Bring to the boil, then lower the heat and simmer gently for 3 minutes, stirring occasionally, until thickened. Serve in individual bowls, sprinkled with sesame seeds.

Nutritional Notes

Per Portion

Energy	335Kcals/1395KJ
Fat	11.5g
Saturated Fat	2g
Cholesterol	5mg

Trail Mix

Eat this nutritious snack on the run, or sprinkle it on top of yogurt or stewed fruit. It makes an excellent nibble between meals, but is quite high in calories, so don't get too carried away with it!

Ingredients

Makes 250g/9oz/scant 2 cups

50g/2oz/⅓ cup ready-to-eat dried apricots or figs, quartered
50g/2oz/⅓ cup raisins or sultanas
50g/2oz/½ cup hazelnuts
50g/2oz/scant ½ cup sunflower seeds
50g/2oz/scant ½ cup pumpkin seeds

1 Cut the apricots or figs into quarters and place in a large bowl.

2 Add all the remaining ingredients and toss everything together. Store in an airtight container and use within 2–3 weeks.

Cook's Tip

Other dried fruits or nuts may be added or substituted for those already present in the mix. Both nuts and seeds have a high oil content so will turn rancid quite quickly. Be sure to use them fresh.

Nutritional Notes

Per 15ml/1 tbsp Portion

Energy	70Kcals/285KJ
Fat	5g
Saturated Fat	1g
Cholesterol	0

Crunchy Fruit Layer

INGREDIENTS

Serves 2

1 peach or nectarine
75g/3oz/1 cup crunchy toasted oat cereal
150ml/¼ pint/⅔ cup low-fat natural yogurt
15ml/1 tbsp pure fruit jam
15ml/1 tbsp unsweetened fruit juice

NUTRITIONAL NOTES
Per Portion

Energy	240Kcals/1005KJ
Fat	3g
Saturated Fat	1g
Cholesterol	3mg

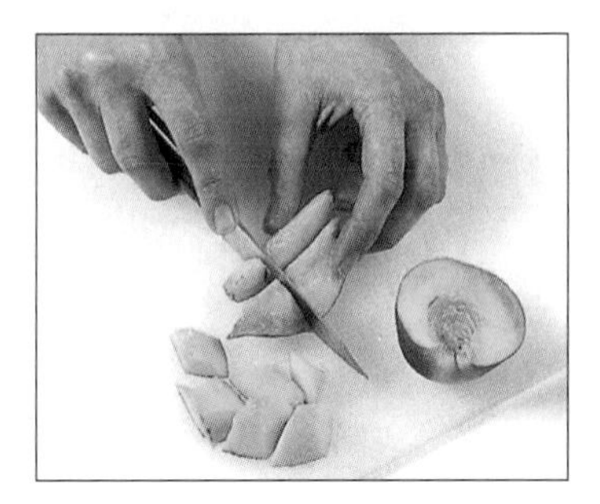

1 Remove the stone from the peach or nectarine and cut the fruit into bite-size pieces with a sharp knife.

2 Divide the chopped fruit between two tall glasses, reserving a few pieces for decoration.

3 Sprinkle the oat cereal over the fruit in an even layer, then top with the yogurt.

4 Stir the jam and fruit juice together in a jug, then drizzle the mixture over the yogurt. Decorate with the reserved peach or nectarine and serve at once.

COOK'S TIP

If you prefer to use a flavoured toasted oat cereal (raisin and almond, perhaps, or tropical fruits) be sure to check the nutritional information on the label and choose the variety with the lowest amount of added sugar. Any fruit jam and juice which complement each other and the chosen fruit can be used.

Apricot and Almond Muesli

There is no added sugar in this wholewheat fruit and nut muesli, which is packed with fibre, vitamins and minerals.

INGREDIENTS

Serves 8

50g/2oz/½ cup whole blanched almonds
115g/4oz/⅔ cup ready-to-eat dried apricots
200g/7oz/2 cups whole rolled oats
75g/3oz/2 cups wheatflakes or oatbran flakes
50g/2oz/⅓ cup raisins or sultanas
40g/1½oz/⅓ cup pumpkin seeds
40g/1½oz/⅓ cup sunflower seeds
skimmed milk, low-fat natural yogurt or fresh fruit juice, and fresh fruit, to serve

1 Using a sharp knife, carefully cut the almonds into slivers.

2 Cut the dried apricots into small even-size pieces.

3 Stir all the ingredients together in a large bowl. Store in an airtight container and use within 6 weeks.

4 Serve with skimmed milk, natural low-fat yogurt or fruit juice and top with fresh fruit, such as peach, banana or strawberry slices.

COOK'S TIP

Ring the changes by adding other dried fruits, such as chopped dates, figs, peaches, pear, pineapple or apple chunks. Walnuts, brazil nuts or hazelnuts could be substituted for the almonds.

NUTRITIONAL NOTES

Per Portion (without topping)

Energy	275Kcals/1150KJ
Fat	11g
Saturated Fat	2g
Cholesterol	0

SNACKS AND LIGHT MEALS

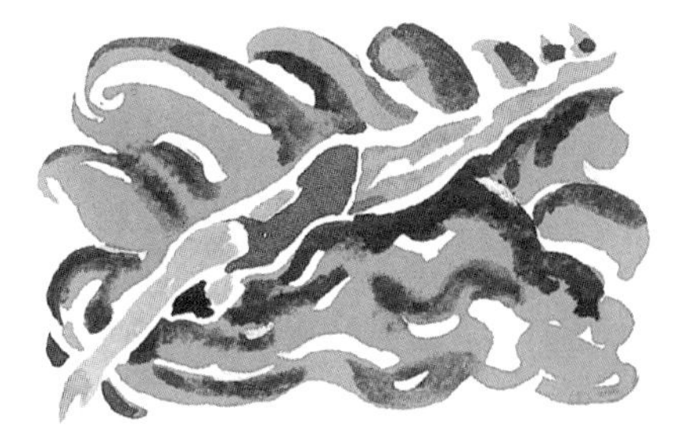

Whatever your lifestyle, whether you are out at work during the day or busy at home, there's likely to be at least one daily meal occasion when you just want something quick and easy to eat. Don't reach for a chocolate bar or pastry. The recipes in this chapter provide appetizing, yet fast ideas that are satisfying and wholesome. Home-made soup with a hunk of wholegrain bread is perfect for a snatched lunch, or try some more unusual sandwich or jacket potato ideas. Go wild with exciting salad combinations, borrow inspiration from foreign cuisines and widen your appreciation of vegetarian dishes.

Spicy Tomato and Lentil Soup

INGREDIENTS

Serves 4

15ml/1 tbsp sunflower oil
1 onion, finely chopped
1–2 garlic cloves, crushed
2.5cm/1in piece of fresh root ginger, peeled and finely chopped
5ml/1 tsp cumin seed, crushed
450g/1lb ripe tomatoes, peeled, seeded and chopped
115g/4oz/2/3 cup red split lentils
1.2 litres/2 pints/5 cups vegetable or chicken stock
15ml/1 tbsp tomato purée
salt and ground black pepper
low-fat natural yogurt and chopped fresh parsley, to garnish (optional)

1 Heat the sunflower oil in a large heavy-based saucepan and cook the chopped onion gently for about 5 minutes until softened.

2 Stir in the garlic, ginger and cumin, followed by the tomatoes and lentils. Cook over a low heat for a further 3–4 minutes.

3 Stir in the stock and tomato purée. Bring to the boil, then lower the heat and simmer gently for about 30 minutes until the lentils are soft. Season to taste with salt and pepper.

4 Purée the soup in a blender or food processor. Return to the clean pan and reheat gently. Serve in heated bowls. Garnish each portion with a swirl of yogurt, if liked, and sprinkle over a little chopped parsley.

NUTRITIONAL NOTES
Per Portion

Energy	165Kcals/695KJ
Fat	4g
Saturated Fat	0.5g
Cholesterol	0

Chunky Bean and Vegetable Soup

A substantial soup, not unlike minestrone, using a selection of vegetables, with cannellini beans for extra protein and fibre. Serve with a hunk of wholegrain bread.

Ingredients

Serves 4

30ml/2 tbsp olive oil
2 celery sticks, chopped
2 leeks, sliced
3 carrots, sliced
2 garlic cloves, crushed
400g/14oz can chopped tomatoes with basil
1.2 litres/2 pints/5 cups vegetable stock
425g/15oz can cannellini beans (or mixed pulses), drained
15ml/1 tbsp pesto sauce
salt and ground black pepper
shavings of Parmesan cheese, to serve

Cook's Tip

Extra vegetables can be added to the soup to make it even more substantial. For example, add some thinly sliced courgettes or finely shredded cabbage for the last 5 minutes of the cooking time. Or, stir in some small wholewheat pasta shapes, if you like. Add them at the same time as the tomatoes, as they will take 10–15 minutes to cook.

1 Heat the olive oil in a large saucepan. Add the celery, leeks, carrots and garlic and cook gently for about 5 minutes until softened.

2 Stir in the tomatoes and the stock. Bring to the boil, then cover and cook gently for 15 minutes.

3 Stir in the beans and pesto, with salt and pepper to taste. Heat through for a further 5 minutes. Serve in heated bowls, sprinkled with shavings of Parmesan cheese.

Nutritional Notes

Per Portion

Energy	205Kcals/855KJ
Fat	11.5g
Saturated Fat	3g
Cholesterol	8.5mg

Provençal Pan Bagna

A wholemeal French baguette, filled with salad and sardines, provides protein, fibre, vitamins and minerals and gives a completely new meaning to the term "packed lunch".

Ingredients

Serves 3

1 wholemeal baguette or 3 large wholemeal rolls
2 garlic cloves, crushed
45ml/3 tbsp olive oil
1 small onion, thinly sliced
2 tomatoes, sliced
7.5cm/3in length of cucumber, sliced
115g/4oz canned sardines in tomato sauce
30ml/2 tbsp chopped fresh parsley
ground black pepper

1 Cut the baguette into three equal pieces, then slice each piece in half lengthways. If using rolls, split them in half. Squash down the crumb on the inside of the bread to make a shallow hollow for the filling. Mix the garlic with the oil, then brush over the inside of the bread.

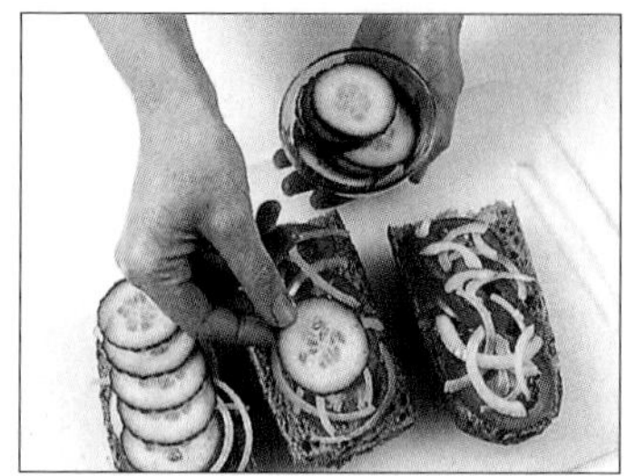

2 Lay slices of onion, tomato and cucumber on one half of the bread. Top with the sardines in tomato sauce. If you are concerned about the bones in the fish, you could slice open the sardines and remove the larger pieces but it makes sound nutritional sense to leave them, as they are edible and are an excellent source of calcium.

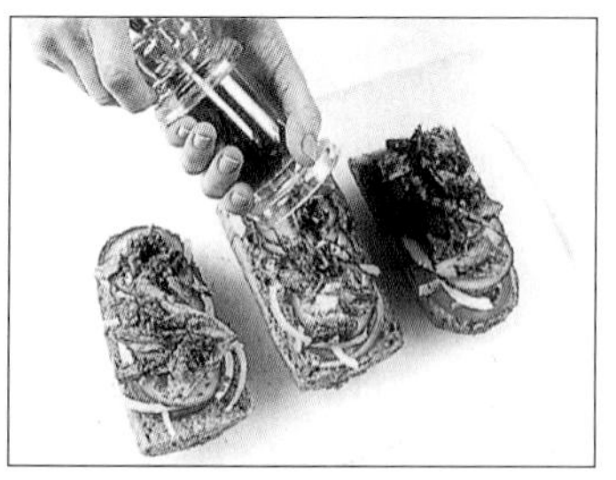

3 Sprinkle the parsley over the fish and season with pepper. Sandwich the bread halves back together and wrap tightly in foil or clear film. Chill for at least 30 minutes before eating.

Nutritional Notes

Per Portion

Energy	320Kcals/1340KJ
Fat	17.5g
Saturated Fat	3.5g
Cholesterol	30.5mg

Guacamole Pitta Pocket

Although they have a reputation for being high in fats and calories, avocados are very nutritious. The high oil content is mainly mono-unsaturated and they are rich in vitamin A.

INGREDIENTS

Serves 2

2 wholewheat pitta breads
10ml/2 tsp Tabasco sauce or chilli sauce (optional)
crisp lettuce, shredded

For the guacamole

1 large ripe avocado
juice of ½ lemon
1 garlic clove, crushed
15ml/1 tbsp finely chopped fresh coriander
2 tomatoes, roughly chopped
5cm/2in length of cucumber, diced
salt and ground black pepper

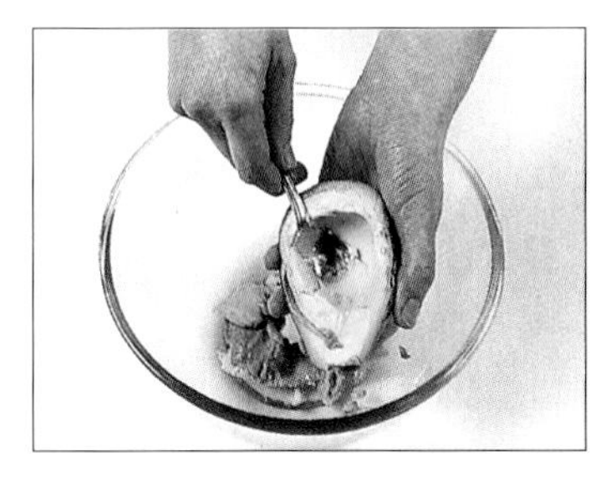

1 Make the guacamole. Cut the avocado in half, remove the stone and scoop out the flesh into a bowl. Chop the flesh roughly, sprinkle it with the lemon juice, then mash, leaving the flesh slightly chunky.

2 Stir in the garlic and coriander. Add the tomatoes and cucumber, with salt and pepper to taste, and mix.

COOK'S TIP

Do not toast the pitta breads – the aim is simply to refresh them.

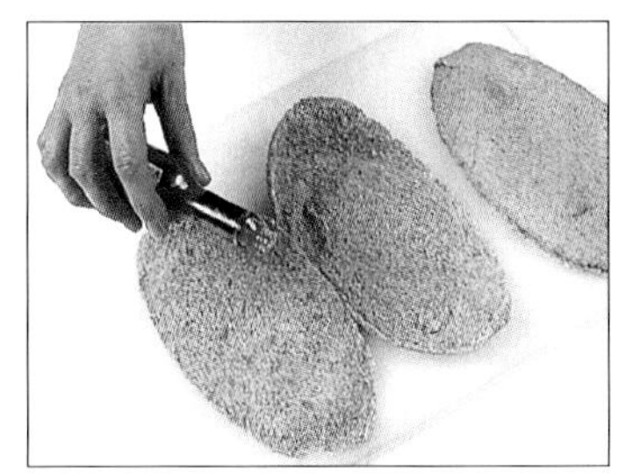

3 Warm the pitta breads briefly in a warm oven or toaster, then slit them open lengthways and open them out to reveal the pockets. Sprinkle a little Tabasco sauce or chilli sauce on the inside, if liked.

4 Half fill the pitta pockets with lettuce, then spoon the guacamole on top. Serve immediately.

NUTRITIONAL NOTES

Per Portion

Energy	345Kcals/1445KJ
Fat	21g
Saturated Fat	3g
Cholesterol	0

Courgette and Potato Tortilla

Ingredients

Serves 4

450g/1lb potatoes, peeled and diced
30ml/2 tbsp olive oil
1 onion, finely chopped
1 garlic clove, crushed
2 courgettes, thinly sliced
30ml/2 tbsp chopped fresh tarragon
4 size 2 eggs, beaten
salt and ground black pepper

Nutritional Notes *Per Portion*	
Energy	265Kcals/1100KJ
Fat	14.5g
Saturated Fat	3g
Cholesterol	231mg

1 Cook the potatoes in boiling, salted water for about 5 minutes.

2 Heat the oil in a large frying pan which can also be used under the grill. Add the onion and cook gently for 3–4 minutes until it is beginning to soften. Add the potatoes, garlic and courgettes to the pan. Cook for about 5 minutes more, shaking the pan occasionally to prevent the potatoes from sticking to the bottom, until the courgettes are softened and the potatoes are lightly browned.

3 Stir the tarragon into the eggs and season with salt and pepper. Pour the eggs over the vegetables in the pan and cook over a moderate heat until the underside of the tortilla is set. Meanwhile, preheat the grill.

4 Place the pan under the grill and cook for a few minutes more until the top of the tortilla has set. Cut into wedges and serve from the pan.

Chicken and Pesto Jackets

Although it is usually served with pasta, pesto also gives a wonderful lift to rice, bread and potato dishes – all good starchy carbohydrates. Here, it is combined with chicken and yogurt to make a low-fat topping for jacket potatoes.

Ingredients

Serves 4

4 baking potatoes, pricked
2 boned chicken breasts
250ml/8fl oz/1 cup low-fat natural yogurt
15ml/1 tbsp pesto sauce
fresh basil, to garnish

1 Preheat the oven to 200°C/400°F/Gas 6. Bake the potatoes for about 1¼ hours, or until they are soft on the inside when tested with a knife.

2 About 20 minutes before the potatoes are ready, cook the chicken breasts, leaving the skin on, so that the flesh remains moist. Either bake the breasts in a dish alongside the potatoes in the oven, or cook them on a rack under a moderately hot grill.

3 Stir together the yogurt and pesto. When the potatoes are cooked through, cut them open. Skin the chicken breasts.

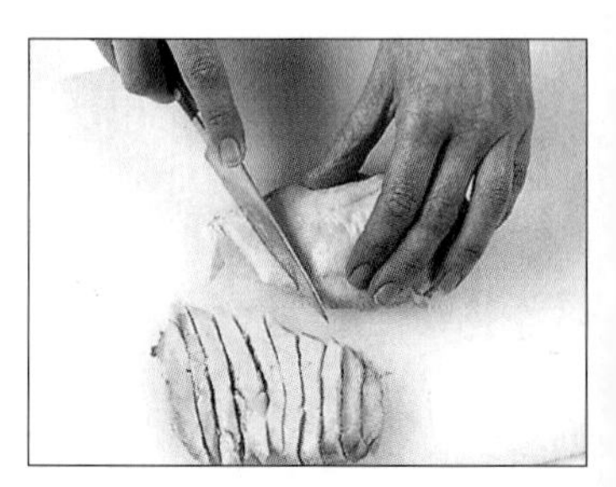

4 Slice the chicken, then fill the potatoes with the slices, top with the yogurt and garnish with basil.

Nutritional Notes *Per Portion*	
Energy	310Kcals/1295KJ
Fat	5.5g
Saturated Fat	1.5g
Cholesterol	35.5mg

Two Pear Salad

Ingredients

Serves 4
2 courgettes, grated
2 avocados
2 ripe eating pears
1 large carrot

For the dressing
250ml/8fl oz/1 cup low-fat natural yogurt
60ml/4 tbsp reduced-calorie mayonnaise
grated rind of 1 lemon
8–10 chives, snipped
30ml/2 tbsp chopped fresh mint
ground black pepper
4 mint sprigs, to garnish

1 Pile the grated courgettes on to four individual serving plates.

2 Cut the avocados in half, then remove the stones and peel. Slice each half lengthways. Core and slice the pears. Arrange avocado and pear slices on top of each courgette salad.

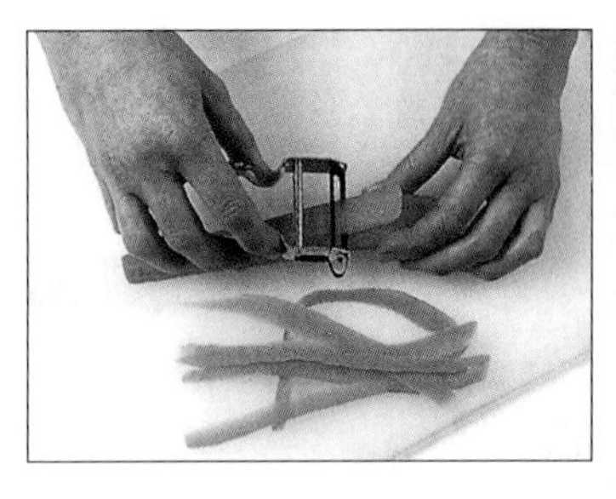

3 Peel the carrot, then use the peeler to peel off fine ribbons.

4 Make the dressing. Mix the yogurt and mayonnaise together in a bowl, then stir in the lemon rind, chives and chopped mint. Season with pepper. Drizzle some of the dressing over each salad and garnish with a mint sprig. Serve immediately.

Cook's Tip

If the salad is not to be served straight away, sprinkle the avocado with lemon juice or the flesh will discolour.

Nutritional Notes
Per Portion

Energy	260Kcals/1090KJ
Fat	19.5g
Saturated Fat	3g
Cholesterol	2.5g

Four Seasons Salad Platter

Fresh vegetable salads are packed with vitamin C. Include some protein foods and serve with a hunk of fresh wholemeal bread for a well-balanced snack or simple lunch.

INGREDIENTS

Serves 2

4 chicory leaves
115g/4oz French beans, lightly cooked
7.5cm/3in length of cucumber, cut into sticks
6 cherry tomatoes
1 hard-boiled egg, halved

Carrot and Radish Salad
2 carrots
2 radishes
15ml/1 tbsp chopped mixed nuts

Beetroot and Onion Salad
2–3 cooked beetroot, sliced
15ml/1 tbsp balsamic or wine vinegar
2–3 spring onions, finely chopped
30ml/2 tbsp chopped fresh parsley

Mushroom and Thyme Salad
75g/3oz/¾ cup button mushrooms, sliced
30ml/2 tbsp lemon juice
15ml/1 tbsp chopped fresh thyme

Tuna and Haricot Bean Salad
90g/3½oz can tuna in oil
200g/7oz can haricot beans
½ red onion, thinly sliced
30ml/2 tbsp chopped fresh parsley

NUTRITIONAL NOTES
Per Portion (including bread)

Energy	405Kcals/1690KJ
Fat	13.5g
Saturated Fat	2.5g
Cholesterol	122.5mg

1 Grate the carrots and radishes. Mix together with the nuts in a bowl.

2 Sprinkle the beetroot with vinegar, add the spring onions and parsley and toss lightly.

3 Mix the mushrooms with the lemon juice and thyme.

4 Drain the tuna and beans, tip them both into a bowl and toss with the onion and parsley.

5 Divide the chicory leaves between two large salad plates. Add a portion of each salad, arranging them attractively with the French beans, cucumber sticks, tomatoes and egg halves. Serve with wholemeal bread.

Stuffed Vine Leaves

Based on the Greek dolmas (or dolmades) but with a wholegrain vegetarian stuffing, this makes an excellent low-fat, high-fibre starter, snack or buffet dish.

Ingredients

Makes about 40

15ml/1 tbsp sunflower oil
5ml/1 tsp sesame oil
1 onion, finely chopped
225g/8oz/1⅓ cups brown rice
600ml/1 pint/2½ cups vegetable stock
1 small yellow pepper, seeded and finely chopped
115g/4oz/⅔ cup ready-to-eat dried apricots, finely chopped
2 lemons
50g/2oz/½ cup pine nuts
45ml/3 tbsp chopped fresh parsley
30ml/2 tbsp chopped fresh mint
2.5ml/½ tsp mixed spice
225g/8oz packet vine leaves preserved in brine, drained
30ml/2 tbsp olive oil
ground black pepper
lemon wedges, to garnish

To serve

300ml/½ pint/1¼ cups low-fat natural yogurt
30ml/2 tbsp chopped fresh mixed herbs
cayenne pepper

Cook's Tip

If vine leaves are not available, the leaves of Swiss chard, young spinach or cabbage can be used instead.

Nutritional Notes

Per Stuffed Vine Leaf

Energy	45Kcals/190KJ
Fat	2g
Saturated Fat	0.5g
Cholesterol	trace

1 Heat the sunflower and sesame oils together in a fairly large saucepan. Add the onion and cook gently for 5 minutes to soften.

2 Add the rice, stirring to coat the grains in oil. Pour in the stock, bring to the boil, then lower the heat, cover the pan and simmer for 30 minutes, or until the rice is tender but retains a little "bite".

3 Stir in the chopped pepper and apricots, with a little more stock if necessary. Replace the lid and cook for a further 5 minutes.

4 Grate 1 lemon, then squeeze both lemons. Drain off any stock which has not been absorbed by the rice. Stir in the pine nuts, herbs, mixed spice, lemon rind and half the juice. Season with pepper and set aside.

5 Bring a saucepan of water to the boil and blanch the vine leaves for 5 minutes. Drain the leaves well, then lay them shiny side down on a board. Cut out any coarse stalks.

6 Place a heap of the rice mixture in the centre of each vine leaf. Fold the stem end over, then the sides and pointed end to make neat parcels. Pack the parcels closely together in a shallow serving dish. Mix the remaining lemon juice with the olive oil. Pour the mixture over the vine leaves, cover and chill before serving. Garnish with lemon wedges. Spoon the yogurt into a bowl, stir in the chopped herbs and sprinkle with a little cayenne. Serve with the stuffed vine leaves.

Mango, Prawn and Tomato Vinaigrette

Ingredients

Serves 4

1 large mango
225g/8oz extra large cooked tiger prawns, peeled and deveined
16 cherry tomatoes, halved
fresh mint, to garnish

For the dressing

15ml/1 tbsp white wine vinegar
2.5ml/½ tsp clear honey
15ml/1 tbsp mango or apricot chutney
15ml/1 tbsp chopped fresh mint
15ml/1 tbsp chopped fresh lemon balm
45ml/3 tbsp olive oil
salt and ground black pepper

Nutritional Notes	
Per Portion	
Energy	230Kcals/960KJ
Fat	10g
Saturated Fat	1.5g
Cholesterol	45.5mg

1 Using a sharp knife, peel, stone and dice the mango carefully. Mix with the tiger prawns and cherry tomatoes in a bowl. Toss lightly to mix, then cover and chill.

2 Make the salad dressing by mixing the vinegar, clear honey, chutney and fresh herbs in a bowl. Gradually whisk in the oil, then add salt and pepper to taste.

3 Spoon the prawn mixture into the dressing and toss lightly, then divide among serving dishes. Garnish with the fresh mint sprigs and serve.

Cook's Tip

If you use frozen prawns, thaw them in a colander, then drain thoroughly on kitchen paper before use or the water will dilute the salad dressing and spoil the flavour.

Chicken Salad with Cranberry Dressing

Ingredients

Serves 4

4 boned chicken breasts, total weight about 675g/1½lb
300ml/½ pint/1¼ cups stock or a mixture of stock and white wine
fresh herb sprigs
200g/7oz mixed salad leaves
50g/2oz/½ cup chopped walnuts or hazelnuts

For the dressing

30ml/2 tbsp olive oil
15ml/1 tbsp walnut or hazelnut oil
15ml/1 tbsp raspberry or red wine vinegar
30ml/2 tbsp cranberry relish
salt and ground black pepper

1 Skin the chicken breasts. Pour the stock (or stock and wine mixture) into a large shallow saucepan. Add the herbs and bring the liquid to simmering point. Poach the chicken breasts for about 15 minutes until cooked through. Alternatively, leave the skin on the breasts and grill or roast them until tender, then remove the skin.

2 Arrange the salad leaves on four plates. Slice each chicken breast neatly, keeping the slices together, then place each breast on top of a portion of salad, fanning the slices out slightly.

3 Make the dressing by shaking all the ingredients together in a screw-top jar. Spoon a little dressing over each salad and sprinkle with the walnuts or hazelnuts.

Nutritional Notes	
Per Portion	
Energy	365Kcals/1530KJ
Fat	22g
Saturated Fat	3.5g
Cholesterol	64.5mg

Mushroom, Leek and Cashew Nut Risotto

Ingredients

Serves 4

225g/8oz/1⅓ cups brown rice
900ml/1½ pints/3¾ cups vegetable stock or a mixture of stock and dry white wine in the ratio 5:1
15ml/1 tbsp walnut or hazelnut oil
2 leeks, sliced
225g/8oz/2 cups mixed wild or cultivated mushrooms, trimmed and sliced
50g/2oz/½ cup cashew nuts
grated rind of 1 lemon
30ml/2 tbsp chopped fresh thyme
25g/1oz/scant ¼ cup pumpkin seeds
salt and ground black pepper
fresh thyme leaves and lemon wedges, to garnish

1 Place the brown rice in a large saucepan, pour in the vegetable stock (or stock and wine), and bring to the boil. Lower the heat and cook gently for about 30 minutes, until all the stock has been absorbed and the rice grains are tender.

2 About 6 minutes before the rice is cooked, heat the oil in a large frying pan, add the leeks and mushrooms and fry over a gentle heat for 3–4 minutes.

3 Add the cashew nuts, lemon rind and chopped thyme to the vegetables and cook for 1–2 minutes more. Season with salt and pepper.

4 Drain off any excess stock from the cooked rice and stir in the vegetable mixture. Turn into a serving dish. Scatter the pumpkin seeds over the top and garnish with the fresh thyme sprigs and lemon wedges. Serve at once.

Nutritional Notes

Per Portion

Energy	395Kcals/1645KJ
Fat	14g
Saturated Fat	2.5g
Cholesterol	0

Fattoush

This Middle-Eastern mixed salad is traditionally topped with pieces of unleavened bread to soak up the dressing. It provides the perfect solution of what to do with slightly stale pitta breads.

INGREDIENTS

Serves 4

2 wholemeal pitta breads
1 iceberg or cos lettuce, torn into pieces
1 green pepper, seeded
10cm/4in length of cucumber
4 tomatoes
4 spring onions
a few black olives, to garnish

For the dressing

60ml/4 tbsp olive oil
45ml/3 tbsp freshly squeezed lemon juice
2 garlic cloves, crushed
45ml/3 tbsp finely chopped fresh parsley
30ml/2 tbsp finely chopped fresh mint
few drops of harissa or chilli sauce (optional)
salt and ground black pepper

COOK'S TIP

Any salad leaves can be used instead of lettuce. Try young spinach leaves or Swiss chard for a change.

1 Grill or toast the pitta breads on both sides until crisp and golden. Cut into rough squares and set aside.

2 Place the lettuce in a large bowl. Chop the green pepper, cucumber, tomatoes and spring onions roughly, making sure they are all about the same size. Add them to the lettuce and toss together well.

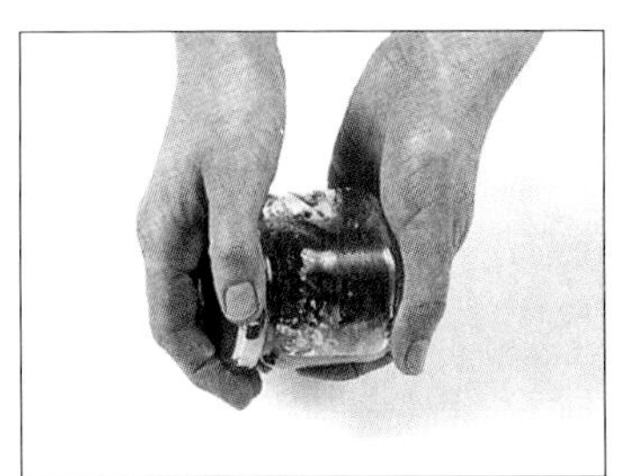

3 Make the dressing by shaking all the ingredients together in a screw-top jar.

4 Just before serving the dish, pour the dressing from the jar over the salad and toss well to combine together. Scatter pieces of pitta bread over the salad and garnish with the black olives.

NUTRITIONAL NOTES

Per Portion

Energy	225Kcals/935KJ
Fat	13g
Saturated Fat	2g
Cholesterol	0

Salmon and Tuna Parcels

You need fairly large smoked salmon slices as they are wrapped around a light tuna mixture before being served on a vibrant salad. Kiwi fruit is a particularly rich source of vitamin C.

INGREDIENTS

Serves 4

30ml/2 tbsp low-fat natural yogurt
15ml/1 tbsp sun-dried tomato paste
5ml/1 tsp wholegrain honey mustard
grated rind and juice of 1 lime
200g/7oz can tuna in brine, drained
130g/4½oz smoked salmon slices
fresh mint leaves, to garnish
ground black pepper

For the salad

3 tomatoes, sliced
2 kiwi fruit, peeled and sliced
¼ cucumber, cut into julienne sticks
15ml/1 tbsp chopped fresh mint
45ml/3 tbsp vinaigrette dressing

> COOK'S TIP
>
> Although healthy eating guidelines recommend reducing the amount of fat (particularly saturated fat) in the diet, salad dressings made with poly-unsaturated or mono-unsaturated oil, such as olive oil, can and should be included, in sensible moderation. This recipe is not high in calories, but if weight control is a real issue, use an oil-free dressing instead of vinaigrette.

1 Mix the yogurt, tomato paste and mustard in a bowl. Stir in the grated lime rind and juice. Add the tuna, with black pepper to taste, and mix well.

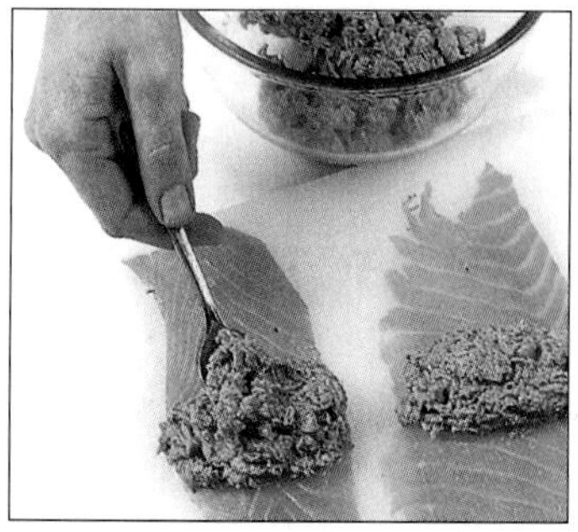

2 Spread out the salmon slices on a board and spoon some of the tuna mixture on to each piece.

3 Roll up or fold the smoked salmon into neat parcels. Carefully press the edges together to seal.

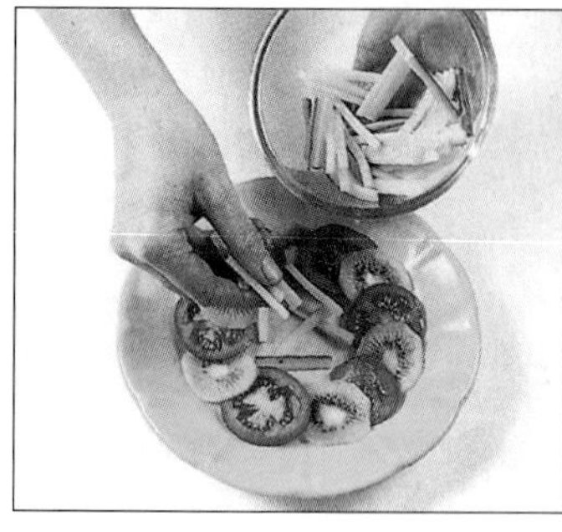

4 Make the salad. Arrange the tomato and kiwi slices on four serving plates. Scatter over the cucumber sticks. Add the chopped mint to the vinaigrette dressing and spoon a little over each salad.

5 Arrange 3–4 salmon parcels on each salad, garnish with the mint leaves and serve.

NUTRITIONAL NOTES

Per Portion

Energy	200Kcals/835KJ
Fat	11.5g
Saturated Fat	2g
Cholesterol	33.5mg

Eggs en Cocotte

Ingredients

Serves 4

4 eggs
20ml/4 tsp freshly grated Parmesan cheese
chopped fresh parsley, to garnish

For the ratatouille

1 small red pepper
15ml/1 tbsp olive oil
1 onion, finely chopped
1 garlic clove, crushed
2 courgettes, diced
400g/14oz can chopped tomatoes with basil
salt and ground black pepper

1 Using a sharp vegetable knife, cut the red pepper in half on a board and remove the seeds. Then cut the red pepper into dice. Preheat the oven to 190°C/375°F/Gas 5.

2 Heat the oil in a frying pan. Add the onion, garlic, courgettes and pepper and sauté over moderate heat for 3–4 minutes until softened. Stir in the tomatoes, with salt and pepper to taste, and cook gently for 5 minutes.

3 Divide the ratatouille among four individual ovenproof dishes or large ramekins, each with a capacity of about 300ml/½ pint/1¼ cups.

4 Make a small hollow in the centre of each and break in an egg.

5 Grind some black pepper over the top of each cocotte and sprinkle with the Parmesan cheese. Bake for 10–15 minutes until the eggs are set. Sprinkle with the fresh parsley and serve at once.

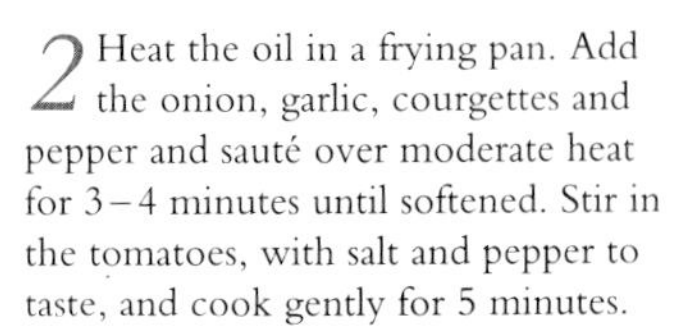

Nutritional Notes

Per Portion

Energy	150Kcals/625KJ
Fat	10g
Saturated Fat	3g
Cholesterol	214.5mg

Mushroom and Fennel Hotpot

Marvellous flavours permeate this unusual vegetarian main course or accompaniment. Mushrooms provide useful amounts of vitamins, minerals and fibre.

Ingredients

Serves 4

25g/1oz dried shiitake mushrooms
1 small head of fennel or 4 celery sticks
30ml/2 tbsp olive oil
12 shallots, peeled
225g/8oz/2 cups button mushrooms, trimmed and halved
300ml/½ pint/1¼ cups dry cider
25g/1oz sun-dried tomatoes
30ml/2 tbsp sun-dried tomato paste
1 bay leaf
chopped fresh parsley, to garnish

Cook's Tip

Dried mushrooms swell up a great deal after soaking, so a little goes a long way both in terms of flavour and quantity.

1 Place the dried mushrooms in a bowl. Pour over boiling water to cover and set aside for 10 minutes.

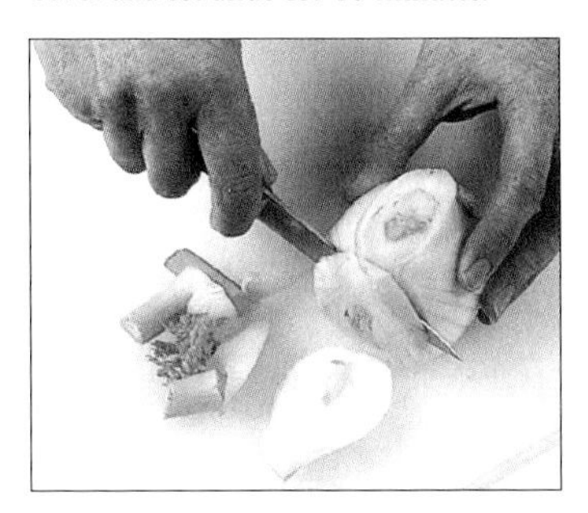

2 Roughly chop the fennel or celery sticks and heat the oil in a flameproof casserole. Add the shallots and fennel or celery and sauté for about 10 minutes over a moderate heat until the mixture is softened and lightly browned. Add the button mushrooms and fry for 2–3 minutes.

3 Drain the dried mushrooms, reserving the liquid. Cut up any large pieces and add to the pan.

Nutritional Notes

Per Portion

Energy	170Kcals/715KJ
Fat	11.5g
Saturated Fat	1.5g
Cholesterol	0

4 Pour in the cider and stir in the sun-dried tomatoes and the paste. Add the bay leaf. Bring to the boil, then lower the heat, cover the casserole and simmer gently for about 30 minutes.

5 If the mixture seems dry, stir in the reserved liquid from the soaked mushrooms. Reheat briefly, then remove the bay leaf and serve, sprinkled with plenty of chopped parsley.

Salads and Vegetable Accompaniments

This chapter includes delicious accompaniments, based on the healthy starchy carbohydrate foods like rice, pasta, pulses and potatoes, as well as recipes for interesting salads and cooked vegetable dishes. Fruit and vegetables provide valuable vitamins, minerals and fibre, essential for a high vitality diet. Your aim should be to include 5–6 portions daily (and this doesn't include potatoes). With such an amazing choice now readily available, this shouldn't be difficult. Shop wisely, buy fresh-looking produce, be adventurous to ensure a good variety and cook with care to preserve nutritional value. Make use of herbs, spices and garlic to tempt even the most fussy of vegetable eaters.

Cracked Wheat Salad with Oranges and Almonds

Bulgar wheat makes an excellent alternative to rice or pasta.

Ingredients

Serves 4

1 small green pepper
150g/5oz/1 cup bulgar wheat
600ml/1 pint/2½ cups water
¼ cucumber, diced
15g/½oz/½ cup chopped fresh mint
40g/1½oz/⅓ cup flaked almonds, toasted
grated rind and juice of 1 lemon
2 seedless oranges
salt and ground black pepper
mint sprigs, to garnish

1 Using a sharp vegetable knife, carefully halve and seed the green pepper. Then cut it on a board into small cubes and put to one side.

2 Place the bulgur wheat in a saucepan and add the water. Bring to the boil, lower the heat, cover and simmer for 10–15 minutes until tender. Alternatively, place the bulgar wheat in a heatproof bowl, pour over boiling water and leave to soak for 30 minutes. Most, if not all, of the water should be absorbed; drain off any excess.

3 Toss the bulgar wheat with the cucumber, green pepper, mint and toasted almonds in a serving bowl. Add the grated lemon rind and juice.

4 Cut the rind from the oranges, then working over the bowl to catch the juice, cut the oranges into neat segments. Add to the bulgar mixture, then season and toss lightly. Garnish with the mint sprigs.

Nutritional Notes

Per Portion

Energy	240Kcals/995KJ
Fat	6.5g
Saturated Fat	0.5g
Cholesterol	0

Fruity Brown Rice Salad

An Oriental-style dressing gives this colourful rice salad extra piquancy. Whole grains like brown rice are unrefined, so they retain their natural fibre, vitamins and minerals.

Ingredients

Serves 4 – 6
115g/4oz/ 2/3 cup brown rice
1 small red pepper, seeded and diced
200g/7oz can sweetcorn niblets, drained
45ml/3 tbsp sultanas
225g/8oz can pineapple pieces in fruit juice
15ml/1 tbsp light soy sauce
15ml/1 tbsp sunflower oil
15ml/1 tbsp hazelnut oil
1 garlic clove, crushed
5ml/1 tsp finely chopped fresh root ginger
ground black pepper
4 spring onions, sliced, to garnish

Cook's Tip

Hazelnut oil gives a wonderfully distinctive flavour to any salad dressing. It is like olive oil, in that it contains mainly mono-unsaturated fats.

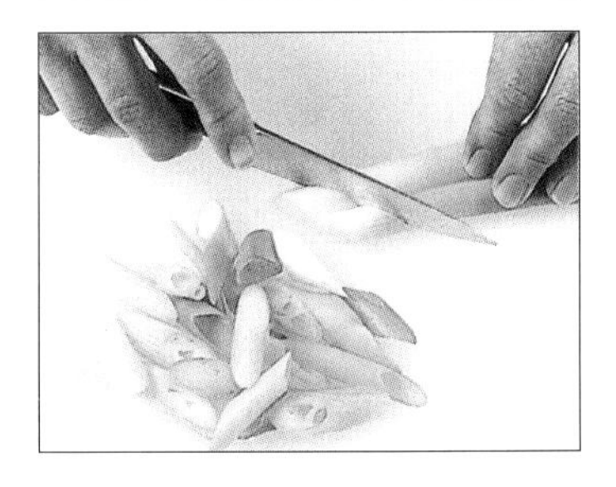

1 Cook the brown rice in a large saucepan of lightly salted boiling water for about 30 minutes, or until it is tender. Drain thoroughly and cool. Meanwhile, prepare the garnish by slicing the spring onions at an angle and setting aside.

2 Tip the rice into a bowl and add the red pepper, sweetcorn and sultanas. Drain the pineapple pieces, reserving the juice, then add them to the rice mixture and toss lightly.

3 Pour the reserved pineapple juice into a clean screw-top jar. Add the soy sauce, sunflower and hazelnut oils, garlic and root ginger. Add some salt and pepper. Then close the jar tightly and shake well to combine.

4 Pour the dressing over the salad and toss well. Scatter the spring onions over the top.

Nutritional Notes

Per Portion

Energy	270Kcals/1125KJ
Fat	7g
Saturated Fat	1g
Cholesterol	0

Cabbage Slaw with Date and Apple

Three types of cabbage are shredded together for serving raw, so that the maximum amount of vitamin C is retained in this cheerful salad.

INGREDIENTS

Serves 6–8
¼ small white cabbage, shredded
¼ small red cabbage, shredded
¼ small Savoy cabbage, shredded
175g/6oz/1 cup dried stoned dates
3 eating apples
juice of 1 lemon
10ml/2 tsp caraway seeds

For the dressing
60ml/4 tbsp olive oil
15ml/1 tbsp cider vinegar
5ml/1 tsp clear honey
salt and ground black pepper

1 Finely shred all the cabbages and place them in a large salad bowl.

2 Chop the dates and add them to the cabbage.

3 Core the eating apples and slice them thinly into a mixing bowl. Add the lemon juice and toss together to prevent discoloration before adding to the salad bowl.

4 Make the dressing. Combine the oil, vinegar and honey in a screw-top jar. Add salt and pepper, then close the jar tightly and shake well. Pour the dressing over the salad, toss lightly, then sprinkle with the caraway seeds and toss again.

NUTRITIONAL NOTES
Per Portion

Energy	200Kcals/835KJ
Fat	8g
Saturated Fat	1g
Cholesterol	0

COOK'S TIP

Support local orchards by looking out for different home-grown apples.

Sprouted Seed Salad

If you sprout beans, lentils and whole grains it increases their nutritional value, and they make a deliciously crunchy salad.

INGREDIENTS

Serves 4
2 eating apples
115g/4oz alfalfa sprouts
115g/4oz beansprouts
115g/4oz aduki beansprouts
¼ cucumber, sliced
1 bunch watercress, trimmed
1 carton mustard and cress, trimmed

For the dressing
150ml/¼ pint/⅔ cup low-fat natural yogurt
juice of ½ lemon
bunch of chives, snipped
30ml/2 tbsp chopped fresh herbs
ground black pepper

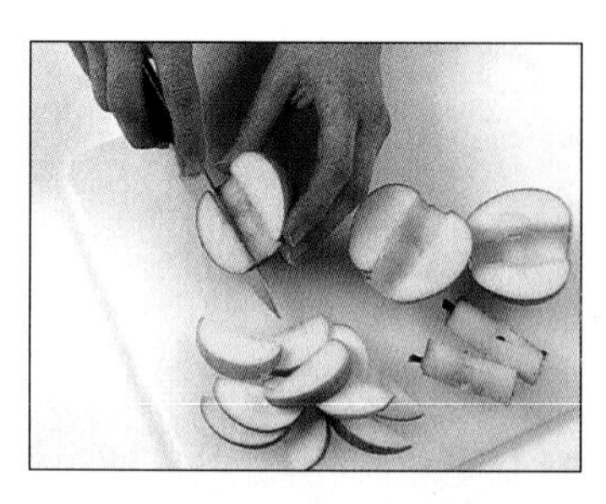

1 Core and slice the apples and mix with the other salad ingredients.

2 Mix the dressing ingredients in a jug. Drizzle over the salad and toss together just before serving.

NUTRITIONAL NOTES
Per Portion

Energy	85Kcals/355KJ
Fat	1.5g
Saturated Fat	0.5g
Cholesterol	1.5mg

Citrus Green Leaf Salad with Croûtons

Wholemeal croûtons add a delicious crunch to leaf salads. The kumquats or orange segments provide a colour contrast as well as a good helping of vitamin C.

Ingredients

Serves 4–6

4 kumquats or 2 seedless oranges
200g/7oz mixed green salad leaves
4 slices of wholemeal bread, crusts removed
30–45ml/2–3 tbsp pine nuts, lightly toasted

For the dressing

grated rind of 1 lemon and 15ml/1tbsp juice
45ml/3 tbsp olive oil
5ml/1 tsp wholegrain mustard
1 garlic clove, crushed

1 Thinly slice the kumquat, or peel and segment the oranges.

Nutritional Notes

Per Portion (if serving 4)

Energy	250Kcals/1000KJ
Fat	15g
Saturated fat	2g
Cholesterol	0

2 Tear all the salad leaves into bite-size pieces and place together in a large salad bowl.

3 Toast the bread on both sides and cut into cubes. Add to the salad leaves with the sliced kumquats or orange segments.

4 Shake all the dressing ingredients together in a jar. Pour over the salad just before serving and scatter the toasted pine nuts over the top.

Mixed Bean Salad with Tomato Dressing

All pulses are a good source of vegetable protein, and minerals.

Ingredients

Serves 4

115g/4oz French beans
425g/15oz can mixed pulses, drained and rinsed
2 celery sticks, finely chopped
1 small onion, finely chopped
3 tomatoes, chopped
45ml/3 tbsp chopped fresh parsley, to garnish

For the dressing

45ml/3 tbsp olive oil
10ml/2 tsp red wine vinegar
1 garlic clove, crushed
15ml/1 tbsp tomato chutney
salt and ground black pepper

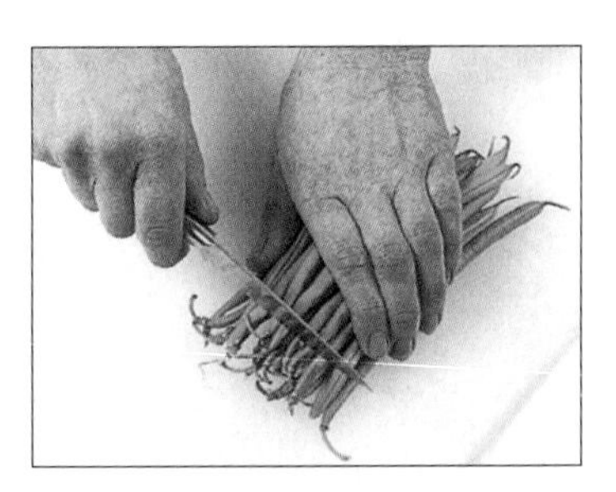

1 Remove the ends from the French beans, then cook the beans in boiling water for 5–6 minutes (or steam for 10 minutes) until tender. Drain, then refresh under cold running water and cut into thirds.

2 Place the French beans and pulses in a large bowl. Add the celery, onion and tomatoes and toss lightly.

3 Shake the dressing ingredients together in a jar. Pour over the salad and sprinkle with the parsley.

Cook's Tip

Cans of mixed pulses include several different types such as chick-peas, pinto, black-eye, red kidney, soya and aduki beans, and save the hassle of long soaking and cooking which dried beans require.

Nutritional Notes

Per Portion

Energy	175Kcals/740KJ
Fat	9.5g
Saturated Fat	1.5g
Cholesterol	0

Baked Mushrooms with Nutty Oat Stuffing

Flat mushrooms, rich in B-group vitamins, have a wonderful flavour and are perfect for this nutty stuffing.

INGREDIENTS

Serves 4

30ml/2 tbsp sunflower oil
8 large flat mushrooms, wiped
1 onion, chopped
1 garlic clove, crushed
25g/1oz/¼ cup porridge oats
225g/8oz can chopped tomatoes with herbs
2.5ml/½ tsp hot pepper sauce
25g/1oz/¼ cup pine nuts
25g/1oz/¼ cup freshly grated Parmesan cheese
salt and ground black pepper

1 Preheat the oven to 190°C/375°F/ Gas 5. Use a little of the oil to grease a shallow ovenproof dish lightly. The dish should be large enough to hold the mushroom caps in a single layer. Remove the mushroom stalks, chop them roughly and set them aside. Reserve the whole caps.

2 Heat the oil in a small saucepan and sauté the onion, garlic and mushroom stalks until softened and lightly browned. Stir in the oats and cook for 1 minute more.

3 Stir in the tomatoes and hot pepper sauce and add salt and pepper to taste. Arrange the mushroom caps, gills uppermost, in the prepared dish. Divide the stuffing mixture between them.

4 Sprinkle the pine nuts and Parmesan cheese over the stuffed mushrooms. Bake for 25 minutes until the mushrooms are tender and the topping is golden brown.

NUTRITIONAL NOTES

Per Portion

Energy	190Kcals/785KJ
Fat	13.5g
Saturated Fat	3g
Cholesterol	6.5mg

Roasted Mediterranean Vegetables

For a really colourful dish, try these vegetables roasted in olive oil with garlic and rosemary. The flavour is wonderfully intense.

INGREDIENTS

Serves 4

1 each red and yellow pepper
2 Spanish onions
2 large courgettes
1 large aubergine or 4 baby aubergines, trimmed
1 fennel bulb, thickly sliced
2 Marmande or beefsteak tomatoes
8 fat garlic cloves
30ml/2 tbsp olive oil
fresh rosemary sprigs
ground black pepper
lemon wedges and black olives, to garnish

1 Halve and seed the peppers, then cut them into large chunks. Peel the onions and cut into thick wedges.

2 Cut the courgettes and aubergine into large chunks.

3 Preheat the oven to 220°C/425°F/ Gas 7. Spread the peppers, onions, courgettes, aubergine and fennel in a lightly oiled, shallow ovenproof dish or roasting tin, or, if liked, arrange in rows to make a colourful design.

4 Cut each tomato in half and place, cut-side up, with the vegetables.

5 Tuck the garlic cloves among the vegetables, then brush them with the olive oil. Place some sprigs of rosemary among the vegetables and grind over some black pepper, particularly on the tomatoes.

6 Roast for 20–25 minutes, turning the vegetables halfway through the cooking time. Serve from the dish or on a flat platter, garnished with lemon wedges. Scatter some black olives over the top.

NUTRITIONAL NOTES
Per Portion

Energy	180Kcals/755KJ
Fat	8g
Saturated Fat	1g
Cholesterol	0

Mixed Vegetables with Aromatic Seeds

A healthy diet should include plenty of vegetables to provide fibre as well as vitamins and minerals. Here, spices transform everyday vegetables.

Ingredients

Serves 4–6

675g/1½lb small new potatoes
1 small cauliflower
175g/6oz French beans
115g/4oz frozen peas
small piece of fresh root ginger
30ml/2 tbsp sunflower oil
10ml/2 tsp cumin seeds
10ml/2 tsp black mustard seeds
30ml/2 tbsp sesame seeds
juice of 1 lemon
ground black pepper
fresh coriander, to garnish (optional)

1 Scrub the potatoes, cut the cauliflower into small florets, and trim and halve the French beans.

2 Cook the vegetables in separate pans of lightly salted boiling water until tender, allowing, 15–20 minutes for the potatoes, 8–10 minutes for the cauliflower and 4–5 minutes for the beans and peas. Drain thoroughly.

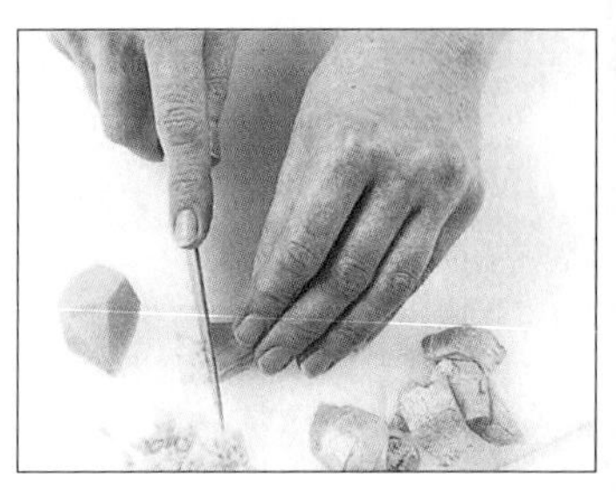

3 Using a small, sharp knife, peel and finely chop the fresh ginger.

4 Heat the oil. Add the ginger and seeds. Fry until they start to pop.

5 Add the vegetables and stir-fry for 2–3 minutes. Sprinkle over the lemon juice and season with pepper. Garnish with coriander, if using.

Cook's Tip

Other vegetables could be used, such as courgettes, leeks or broccoli. Buy whatever looks freshest and do not store vegetables for long periods as their vitamin content will deteriorate.

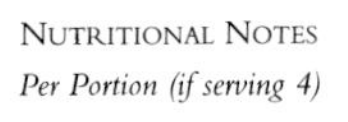

Nutritional Notes

Per Portion (if serving 4)

Energy	285Kcals/1200KJ
Fat	12.5g
Saturated Fat	1.5g
Cholesterol	0

Root Vegetable Casserole

Potatoes, carrots and parsnips are all complex carbohydrates and make a hearty, sustaining vegetable dish, high in fibre and vitamin C. The carrots are also an excellent source of beta-carotene, which is converted to vitamin A in the body.

INGREDIENTS

Serves 4–6

225g/8oz carrots
225g/8oz parsnips
15ml/1 tbsp sunflower oil
knob of butter
15ml/1 tbsp demerara sugar
450g/1lb baby new potatoes, scrubbed
225g/8oz small onions, peeled
400ml/14fl oz/1⅔ cup vegetable stock
15ml/1 tbsp Worcestershire sauce
15ml/1 tbsp tomato purée
5ml/1 tsp wholegrain mustard
2 bay leaves
salt and ground black pepper
chopped parsley, to garnish

COOK'S TIP

Other vegetables could be added, such as leeks, mushrooms, sweet potato or celery. When they are in season, shelled chestnuts make a delicious addition.

1 Peel the carrots and parsnips and cut into large chunks.

2 Heat the oil, butter and sugar in a pan. Stir until the sugar dissolves.

3 Add the potatoes, onions, carrots and parsnips. Sauté for 10 minutes until the vegetables look glazed.

NUTRITIONAL NOTES

Per Portion (if serving 4)

Energy	215Kcals/895KJ
Fat	5.5g
Saturated Fat	1g
Cholesterol	3mg

4 Mix the vegetable stock, Worcestershire sauce, tomato purée and mustard in a jug. Stir well, then pour over the vegetables. Add the bay leaves. Bring to the boil, then lower the heat, cover and cook gently for about 30 minutes until the vegetables are tender.

5 Remove the bay leaves, add salt and pepper to taste and serve, sprinkled with the parsley.

…ENTS 53

Concertina Garlic Potatoes

…w-fat topping these make a superb meal in themselves, or enjoy them as a nutritious accompaniment.

INGREDIENTS

Serves 4

4 large baking potatoes
2 garlic cloves, cut into slivers
60ml/4 tbsp soured cream
60ml/4 tbsp low-fat natural yogurt
30ml/2 tbsp snipped chives
6–8 watercress sprigs, finely chopped (optional)

NUTRITIONAL NOTES
Per Portion

Energy	195Kcals/815KJ
Fat	3.5g
Saturated Fat	2g
Cholesterol	10mg

1 Preheat the oven to 200°C/400°F/Gas 6. Slice each potato several times, cutting almost to the base, so that they retain their shape. Slip garlic between some of the cuts.

COOK'S TIP

The most suitable potatoes for baking are of the floury variety. Some of the best include Estima, Cara, Pentland Squire, Spunta, Kerr's Pink and Record.

2 Place the garlic-filled potatoes in a roasting tin and bake for 1–1¼ hours or until soft when tested with a knife. Meanwhile, mix the soured cream and low-fat yogurt in a bowl. Then stir in the snipped chives, along with the watercress, if using.

3 Serve the baked potatoes on individual plates, with a dollop of the yogurt and cream mixture on top of each.

Potato, Leek and Tomato Bake

INGREDIENTS

Serves 4

675g/1½lb potatoes
2 leeks, trimmed and sliced
3 large tomatoes, sliced
a few fresh rosemary sprigs, crushed
1 garlic clove, crushed
300ml/½ pint/1¼ cups vegetable stock
15ml/1 tbsp olive oil
salt and ground black pepper

NUTRITIONAL NOTES
Per Portion

Energy	180Kcals/740KJ
Fat	3.5g
Saturated Fat	0.5g
Cholesterol	0

1 Preheat the oven to 180°C/350°F/Gas 4 and grease a 1.2 litre/2 pint/5 cup shallow ovenproof dish. Scrub and thinly slice the potatoes. Then layer them with the leeks and tomatoes in the dish, scattering some rosemary between the layers and ending with a layer of potatoes.

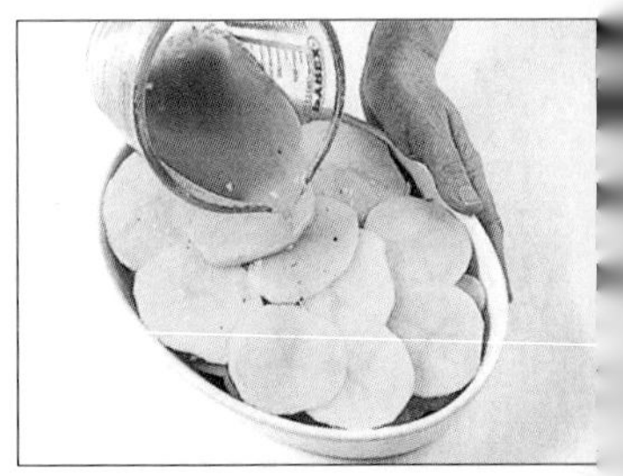

2 Add the garlic to the stock, stir in salt and pepper to taste and pour over the vegetables. Brush the top layer of potatoes with the olive oil.

3 Bake for 1¼–1½ hours until the potatoes are tender and the topping is golden and slightly crisp.

Tomato, Pistachio and Sesame Pilau

INGREDIENTS

Serves 4

3 tomatoes
1 red pepper
225g/8oz/1⅓ cups brown basmati rice
600ml/1 pint/2½ cups vegetable stock or water
pinch of saffron strands soaked in 15ml/1 tbsp boiling water
pinch of salt
4–5 cardamom pods
25g/1oz/¼ cup pistachio nuts, roughly chopped
30ml/2 tbsp sesame seeds, toasted

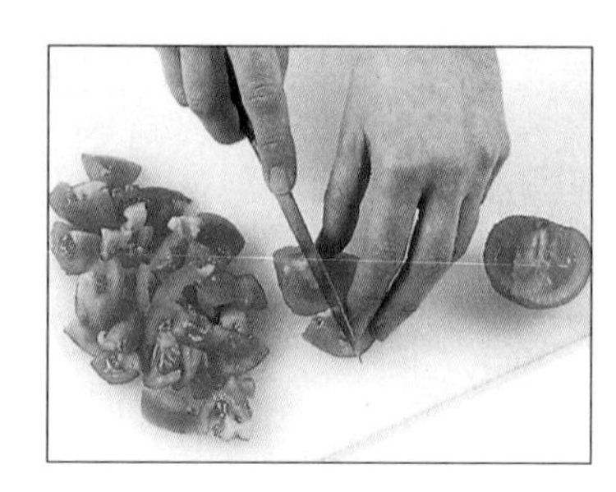

1 Place the tomatoes in boiling water for 30 seconds to loosen the skins, then peel and chop.

2 Using a sharp knife, seed and chop the red pepper.

3 Wash the rice in a sieve under cold running water, then tip into a saucepan. Add the stock or water, soaked saffron liquid and salt. Bring to the boil, then lower the heat, cover and simmer for 25 minutes.

4 Add the tomatoes and peppers to the rice. Crush the cardamom pods, extract the seeds and stir them into the mixture. Cook for a further 5–10 minutes until the rice is tender and all the liquid has been absorbed. If the liquid is absorbed before the rice is cooked, add a little more. It should not be necessary to drain the rice.

5 Tip the rice into a serving dish and scatter the pistachio nuts and sesame seeds over the top.

NUTRITIONAL NOTES
Per Portion

Energy	315Kcals/1310KJ
Fat	10g
Saturated Fat	1.5g
Cholesterol	0

Winter Vegetable Stir-Fry

Brussels sprouts are not always popular, but taste absolutely delicious when steamed and swiftly stir-fried. As a bonus, more of their vitamin B and C content is preserved.

Ingredients

Serves 4
350g/12oz Brussels sprouts
2 courgettes
15ml/1 tbsp sunflower or nut oil
12 shallots, peeled
1 garlic clove, crushed
small piece of fresh root ginger, peeled and finely chopped
25g/1oz/¼ cup walnut pieces

1 If necessary, trim the sprouts and remove any dirty outside leaves.

2 Cut the courgettes into even-size diagonal slices.

3 Steam the Brussels sprouts for about 7–10 minutes, or until they are just tender. Drain, if necessary, and set aside.

4 Heat the oil in a frying pan or wok. Add the shallots and courgettes and stir-fry for 2–3 minutes.

5 Add the sprouts, garlic and ginger and stir-fry for 2 minutes more. Scatter over the walnut pieces, toss them with the vegetable mixture and serve immediately.

Cook's Tip

Choose small, tight Brussels sprouts which don't need to be trimmed or have their outside leaves removed. The darker outside leaves are rich in vitamins and minerals. Shredded cabbage could be used instead of Brussels sprouts, and chestnuts in place of walnuts. Vacuum-packed chestnuts are cooked and ready to use.

Nutritional Notes

Per Portion

Energy	125Kcals/530KJ
Fat	8.5g
Saturated Fat	1g
Cholesterol	0

MAIN MEALS

This chapter contains tempting ideas for meat, poultry, fish and vegetarian meals. The main meal of the day is likely to provide a considerable amount of your daily energy intake, so be sure you're getting good nutritional value for your calories. The meat recipes use lean cuts, and vegetables, dried fruits and pulses are incorporated into the dishes to increase fibre, reduce fat and build in extra vitamins and minerals. Whether cooking for simple midweek meals or special occasions, there's plenty to whet the appetite.

Beef and Broccoli Stir-fry with Black Bean Sauce

INGREDIENTS

Serves 4
15ml/1 tbsp stir-fry oil
225g/8oz lean fillet or rump steak, thinly sliced across the grain
225g/8oz broccoli
115g/4oz baby corn, diagonally halved
45–60ml/3–4 tbsp water
2 leeks, diagonally sliced
227g/8oz can water chestnuts, sliced

For the marinade
15ml/1 tbsp fermented black beans
30ml/2 tbsp dark soy sauce
30ml/2 tbsp Chinese rice vinegar or cider vinegar
15ml/1 tbsp sunflower oil
5ml/1 tsp sugar
2 garlic cloves, crushed
2.5cm/1in piece of fresh root ginger, peeled and finely chopped

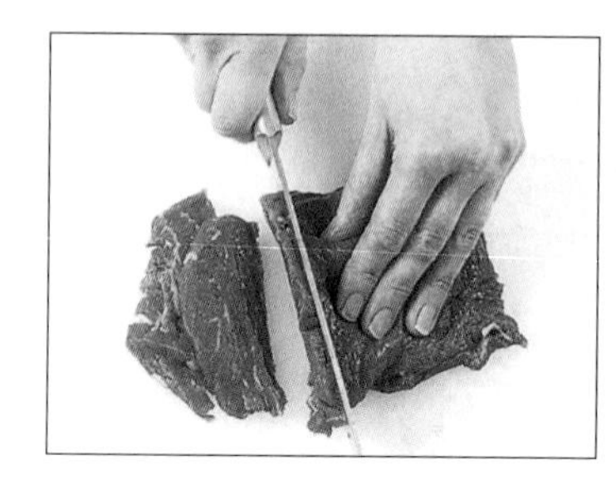

1 Make the marinade. Mash the fermented black beans in a non-metallic bowl. Stir in the remaining ingredients. Cut the steak into thin slices across the grain, then add them to the marinade.

2 Stir the steak well to coat it in the marinade. Cover the bowl and leave for several hours or overnight in the fridge.

3 Heat the stir-fry oil in a large heavy-based frying pan or wok. Drain the steak (reserving the marinade). When the oil is very hot, add the meat and stir-fry for 3–4 minutes. Using a slotted spoon, transfer it to a plate and set aside.

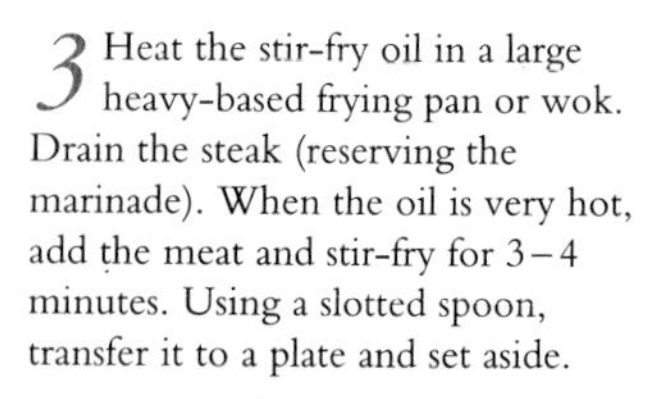

4 Cut the broccoli into small florets. Reheat the oil remaining in the pan, add the broccoli and corn and stir in the water. Cover and steam gently for 5 minutes, or until the vegetables are tender, but still have some "bite".

5 Add the leeks and water chestnuts to the broccoli mixture and toss over the heat for 1–2 minutes. Return the meat to the pan, pour over the reserved marinade and toss the mixture over a high heat.

NUTRITIONAL NOTES
Per Portion

Energy	190Kcals/790KJ
Fat	9g
Saturated Fat	2g
Cholesterol	33.5mg

Beef and Lentil Pies

In this variation of cottage pie, lentils are substituted for some of the meat to produce a dish that is lower in fat and higher in fibre. Some red meat is included to boost the iron content.

INGREDIENTS

Serves 4

175g/6oz/1 cup green lentils
225g/8oz extra lean minced beef
1 onion, chopped
2 celery sticks, chopped
1 large carrot, chopped
1 garlic clove, crushed
425g/15oz can chopped tomatoes
10ml/2 tsp yeast extract
1 bay leaf

For the topping

450g/1lb potatoes, peeled and cut into large chunks
450g/1lb parsnips, peeled and cut into large chunks
60ml/4 tbsp low-fat natural yogurt
45ml/3 tbsp snipped chives
20ml/4 tsp freshly grated Parmesan cheese
2 tomatoes, sliced
25g/1oz/¼ cup pine nuts (optional)

1 Place the lentils in a pan and pour in cold water to cover. Bring to the boil, then boil for 10 minutes.

2 Meanwhile, brown the beef in a saucepan, without any extra fat. Stir in the onion, celery, carrot and garlic. Cook gently for 5 minutes, then stir in the tomatoes.

3 Drain the lentils, reserving 300ml/½ pint/1¼ cups of the cooking water in a measuring jug. Add the lentils to the meat mixture, then dissolve the yeast extract in the cooking water and stir it in. Add the bay leaf, bring to the boil then lower the heat, cover the pan and cook gently for 20 minutes.

4 Make the topping. Bring a saucepan of lightly salted water to the boil and cook the potatoes and parsnips for about 15 minutes, until tender. Drain, tip into a bowl, and mash with the yogurt and chives. Preheat the grill.

5 Remove the bay leaf and divide the mixture among four small dishes. Spoon over the potato mixture. Sprinkle with Parmesan and garnish with tomato slices. Scatter pine nuts over the top, if using, and grill the pies for a few minutes until the topping is crisp and golden.

NUTRITIONAL NOTES
Per Portion

Energy	470Kcals/1970KJ
Fat	10.5g
Saturated Fat	2.5g
Cholesterol	36.5mg

Moroccan Lamb Tagine with Cous-cous

A tagine is a Moroccan stew that typically combines meat and fruit with aromatic herbs and spices. The result is a low-fat casserole with extra vitamins and fibre.

INGREDIENTS

Serves 4

15ml/1 tbsp sunflower oil
350g/12oz lean, boneless lamb, cubed
1 large onion, chopped
1 garlic clove, crushed
600ml/1 pint/2½ cups stock
1 cinnamon stick
small piece of fresh root ginger, peeled and finely chopped
5ml/1 tsp clear honey
grated rind and juice of 1 orange
1 aubergine
4 tomatoes, peeled and chopped
115g/4oz/⅔ cup ready-to-eat dried apricots, halved
30ml/2 tbsp chopped fresh coriander
salt and ground black pepper

For the cous-cous

225g/8oz/1½ cups cous-cous
400ml/14fl oz/1⅔ cups water
pinch of saffron strands, soaked in 15ml/1 tbsp boiling water (optional)
knob of butter
5ml/1 tsp orange flower water (optional)

COOK'S TIP

Cous-cous is a cereal made from ground wheat (semolina) mixed with water and salt and shaped into tiny pellets. Like rice, it can either be served hot with meat, poultry or vegetable dishes, or cold, mixed with nuts and dried fruits for a tasty salad. However, it has the advantage over rice of being extremely quick to cook.

1 Heat the oil in a large saucepan or flameproof casserole. Add the lamb and onion and sauté for 5 minutes until lightly browned.

2 Add the garlic, then stir in the stock, cinnamon, ginger, honey, orange rind and juice. Bring to the boil, then lower the heat, cover the pan and simmer gently for 45 minutes.

3 Meanwhile, wipe the aubergine and cut into pieces. Place them in a mixing bowl. Sprinkle with 30–45ml/2–3 tbsp salt and leave for about 30 minutes so that the bitter juices are drawn out.

4 Add the chopped tomatoes and dried apricots to the casserole. Rinse the aubergines, then drain well and add to the tagine. Cover and cook for a further 45 minutes or until the lamb is tender.

5 About 20 minutes before the lamb is ready, cook the cous-cous, either in a separate pan or in a steamer above the stew. Start by placing the cous-cous in a bowl, pour over lightly salted boiling water to cover and sprinkle with the infused saffron, if using. Soak for 5 minutes. Melt the butter in a saucepan, add the cous-cous and cook over a moderate heat for 3–5 minutes. Alternatively, place the cous-cous in a steamer set above the stew and steam it for 6–7 minutes. Tip the cous-cous into a bowl and sprinkle with orange flower water, if using.

6 Stir the fresh coriander into the tagine just before serving with the cous-cous.

NUTRITIONAL NOTES
Per Portion (with cous-cous)

Energy	430Kcals/1805KJ
Fat	14.5g
Saturated Fat	6g
Cholesterol	75mg

Chilli Lamb and Potato Goulash

INGREDIENTS

Serves 4

450g/1lb lean lamb, cubed
1 onion, roughly chopped
1 garlic clove, crushed
400g/14oz can chopped tomatoes
300ml/½ pint/1¼ cups stock
15ml/1 tbsp tomato chutney
15ml/1 tbsp paprika
2 green chillies, seeded and chopped
450g/1lb small new potatoes, scrubbed
1 red pepper, seeded and chopped
salt and ground black pepper
1 bunch fresh fenugreek leaves (optional)
150g/5oz young spinach leaves

To serve

150ml/¼ pint/⅔ cup low-fat natural yogurt
paprika, for dusting
2 spring onions, chopped

1 Place the lamb in a flameproof casserole over a low heat until the fat runs, then raise the heat and fry until lightly browned. Drain off any excess fat, then add the onion and garlic and sauté for 3–4 minutes until the onions are lightly browned. Add the tomatoes, stock, chutney, paprika and chillies to the casserole. Bring to the boil, then cover and cook gently for 1 hour.

2 Add the potatoes and pepper, replace the lid and cook for a further 20–25 minutes, until the potatoes are tender. Add more stock, if necessary. Season to taste.

3 If using the fenugreek, bring a saucepan of water to the boil, add the bunch of leaves and blanch for 1 minute to remove any bitterness. Drain well and add to the casserole. Tear the spinach leaves into smaller pieces. Add them to the casserole and cook for 5 minutes – the spinach will wilt down rapidly, so don't worry about the large quantity when raw.

4 Serve in individual heated bowls. Spoon a little yogurt over each portion, dust with paprika and scatter over some chopped spring onions.

NUTRITIONAL NOTES

Per Portion (without yogurt topping)

Energy	335Kcals/1410KJ
Fat	11.5g
Saturated Fat	5g
Cholesterol	89mg

Pork with Prunes

Prunes are an excellent source of fibre and beta-carotene. They also provide iron.

INGREDIENTS

Serves 4

225g/8oz/1 cup ready-to-eat prunes, stoned
300ml/½ pint/1¼ cups dry white wine, cider or apple juice
15ml/1 tbsp sunflower oil
4 lean pork steaks
15ml/1 tbsp redcurrant jelly
15ml/1 tbsp cornflour
175ml/6fl oz/¾ cup low-fat natural yogurt
salt and ground black pepper
sprigs of fresh parsley, to garnish
carrots and green vegetables, to serve (optional)

NUTRITIONAL NOTES
Per Portion

Energy	390Kcals/1640KJ
Fat	12.5g
Saturated Fat	4g
Cholesterol	88mg

1 Place the prunes in a mixing bowl and pour over the white wine, cider or apple juice. Leave them to plump up while you cook the pork.

2 Trim the pork steaks by removing any fat. Heat the sunflower oil in a large heavy-based frying pan. Then add the pork and fry until browned on both sides. Drain off any excess fat.

3 Pour in the prunes with the liquid, and add the redcurrant jelly. Season to taste. Bring to the boil, then lower the heat, cover and simmer for about 20 minutes until the pork is tender.

4 Stir the cornflour and yogurt together in a bowl. Using a slotted spoon, transfer the pork and prunes to a warmed serving dish. Cover and keep hot. Gradually add the yogurt mixture to the liquid in the pan, stirring constantly over the heat until the sauce has thickened.

5 Pour the sauce over the pork and prunes and garnish with the parsley sprigs. Serve at once, with carrots and seasonal green vegetables, if you like.

Braised Venison with Orange and Cranberries

Ingredients

Serves 4

675g/1½lb venison
15ml/1 tbsp olive oil
16 shallots, peeled
1 garlic clove, crushed
600ml/1 pint/2½ cups stock
juice of 2 oranges
15ml/1 tbsp orange marmalade
small piece of fresh root ginger, peeled and finely chopped
5ml/1 tsp clear honey
few fresh thyme sprigs
4 large carrots, cut into thick chunks
150g/5oz/1¼ cups fresh cranberries
225g/8oz/2 cups button mushrooms
30ml/2 tbsp chopped walnuts
salt and ground black pepper
fresh thyme sprigs and wholemeal toast croûtes, to garnish

1 Cut the venison into small pieces. Heat the oil in a flameproof casserole and sauté the venison with the whole shallots and the crushed garlic for 5 minutes, or until the shallots are lightly browned.

2 Add the stock, orange juice, marmalade, ginger and honey and stir well.

3 Add the sprigs of thyme and bring to the boil. Then lower the heat, cover the casserole with a lid and cook gently for 1½ hours.

4 Add the carrots, cranberries and mushrooms to the casserole and cook gently for a further 20–30 minutes, or until the venison is tender, adding a little extra stock if necessary.

5 Remove the thyme sprigs and add salt and pepper to taste. Sprinkle the chopped walnuts over the top and garnish with the fresh thyme sprigs and wholemeal toast croûtes.

Nutritional Notes

Per Portion

Energy	365Kcals/1520KJ
Fat	11.5g
Saturated Fat	3g
Cholesterol	143.5mg

Turkey Picadillo

Using minced turkey rather than beef for this Mexican-style dish makes it much lower in fat. Serve as a filling for soft wheat tortillas and then top with some natural low-fat yogurt for a tasty meal. Alternatively, serve as a topping for baked potatoes.

Ingredients

Serves 4

15ml/1 tbsp sunflower oil
1 onion, chopped
450g/1lb minced turkey
1–2 garlic cloves, crushed
1 green chilli, seeded and finely chopped
6 tomatoes, peeled and chopped
15ml/1 tbsp tomato purée or sun-dried tomato paste
2.5ml/½ tsp ground cumin
1 yellow or orange pepper, seeded and chopped
50g/2oz/⅓ cup raisins
50g/2oz/½ cup flaked almonds, toasted
45ml/3 tbsp chopped fresh coriander
150ml/¼ pint/⅔ cup low-fat natural yogurt
2–3 spring onions, finely chopped
4 soft tortillas
salt and ground black pepper
shredded lettuce, to serve

1 Heat the oil in a large frying pan and add the chopped onion. Cook gently for 5 minutes until soft. Then stir in the minced turkey and garlic and cook gently for a further 5 minutes.

2 Stir in the chilli, tomatoes, tomato purée or paste, cumin, yellow or orange pepper and raisins. Cover and cook over a gentle heat for 15 minutes, stirring occasionally and adding a little water if necessary.

3 Stir in the toasted almonds, with about two-thirds of the chopped fresh coriander. Add salt and freshly ground black pepper to taste.

4 Tip the yogurt into a bowl. Stir in the remaining fresh coriander and the spring onions.

5 Heat the tortillas in a dry frying pan, without oil, for 15–20 seconds. Place some shredded lettuce and turkey mixture on each tortilla, roll up like a pancake and transfer to a plate. Top with a generous spoonful of the low-fat yogurt and coriander mixture and serve immediately.

Nutritional Notes
Per Portion

Energy	460Kcals/1920KJ
Fat	12.5g
Saturated Fat	2g
Cholesterol	57mg

Chicken Biryani

A wonderfully spicy baked Indian dish made with brown basmati rice.

INGREDIENTS

Serves 6

30ml/2 tbsp sunflower oil
1 large onion, chopped
2 garlic cloves, crushed
small piece of fresh root ginger, peeled and finely chopped
675g/1½lb boned chicken breasts or thighs, skinned and cubed
6 cardamom pods
10ml/2 tsp ground cumin
10ml/2 tsp ground coriander
2.5ml/½ tsp chilli powder
6 cloves
1 cinnamon stick
2.5ml/½ tsp whole black peppercorns
2 bay leaves
juice of 1 lemon
4 large tomatoes, peeled and chopped
150ml/¼ pint/⅔ cup chicken stock
few drops of rosewater (optional)
low-fat natural yogurt or raita, to serve

For the rice
275g/10oz/1⅔ cups brown basmati rice
30ml/2 tbsp warm milk
pinch of saffron strands
15ml/1 tbsp sunflower oil
1 small onion, thinly sliced
750ml/1¼ pints/3 cups chicken stock
few drops of rosewater (optional)

For the garnish
roughly chopped pistachio nuts
sultanas
fresh coriander sprigs

COOK'S TIP

A minty potato raita is marvellously cooling with the biryani. Spoon 150ml/¼ pint/⅔ cup natural low-fat yogurt into a bowl. Stir in 5ml/1 tsp mint sauce, then add 225g/8oz cooked, cubed potato. Mix gently and sprinkle with a little chilli powder before serving.

1 Preheat the oven to 170°C/325°F/Gas 3. Heat the oil in a frying pan and cook the onion gently for about 5 minutes until softened. Stir in the garlic and ginger and cook for about 1 minute more.

2 Add the chicken cubes to the pan and fry for 2–3 minutes until they turn white. Crush the cardamom pods and extract the seeds. Add these to the frying pan, with the rest of the spices and the bay leaves. Stir over a gentle heat for 1 minute.

3 Add the lemon juice and chopped tomatoes, then stir in the stock. Bring to the boil, then lower the heat, cover and cook gently for 40 minutes.

4 Rinse and drain the rice. Warm the milk in a small pan, stir in the saffron and set aside to infuse. Heat the oil in a pan and fry the onion until soft. Stir in the rice, then add the stock and saffron liquid. Bring to the boil, then cover the pan and simmer for about 30 minutes, until the rice is tender and all the stock is absorbed.

5 Layer the rice and chicken in an ovenproof dish, ending with rice. Cover and bake for about 30 minutes, to allow all the flavours to combine.

6 Stir gently to bring some of the curry to the top. Sprinkle with rosewater, if using, and garnish with the pistachio nuts, sultanas and fresh coriander. Serve with a bowl of yogurt or raita, if liked.

NUTRITIONAL NOTES

Per Portion

Energy	425Kcals/1770KJ
Fat	13.5g
Saturated Fat	3g
Cholesterol	49mg

Chicken, Barley and Apple Casserole

Wholegrain pot barley would give this casserole maximum value in terms of minerals and B-group vitamins, but pearl barley can be used instead.

INGREDIENTS

Serves 4

4 boneless chicken breasts
15ml/1 tbsp sunflower oil
1 large onion, sliced
1 garlic clove, crushed
3 carrots, cut into chunky sticks
2 celery sticks, thickly sliced
115g/4oz/⅔ cup pot or pearl barley
750ml/1¼ pints/3 cups chicken stock
1 bay leaf
few sprigs each of fresh thyme and marjoram
3 eating apples
chopped fresh parsley, to garnish

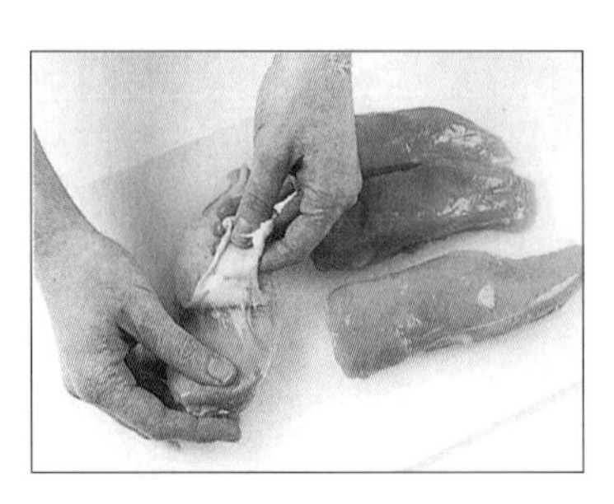

1 Remove the skin from the chicken. Heat the oil and sauté the onion for about 5 minutes until soft.

COOK'S TIP

You can also cook the casserole in a preheated 190°C/375°F/Gas 5 oven. The timings are the same. Chicken thighs are not as "meaty" as chicken breasts, but they are good value for money.

2 Stir in the garlic, carrots and celery and continue to cook over a gentle heat for a further 5 minutes.

3 Stir in the pot or pearl barley, then add the chicken breasts, stock and herbs. Bring to the boil, then lower the heat, cover the casserole and cook gently for 1 hour.

4 Core the apples and slice them thickly. Add to the casserole, replace the lid and cook for 15 minutes more. Sprinkle with the chopped parsley and serve.

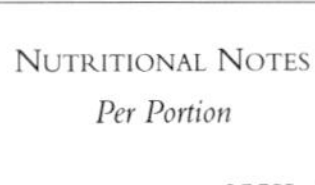

NUTRITIONAL NOTES
Per Portion

Energy	355Kcals/1485KJ
Fat	9g
Saturated Fat	2g
Cholesterol	64.5mg

Chicken, Banana and Pineapple Kebabs

INGREDIENTS

Serves 4

4 boned chicken thighs, skinned and cubed
½ small fresh pineapple
2 firm bananas
fresh orange segments and bay leaves, to garnish

For the marinade

45ml/3 tbsp sunflower oil
15ml/1 tbsp clear honey
5ml/1 tsp French wholegrain mustard
5ml/1 tsp crushed coriander seeds
grated rind and juice of 1 orange
4 cardamom pods

NUTRITIONAL NOTES

Per Portion

Energy	275Kcals/1150KJ
Fat	14.5g
Saturated Fat	3g
Cholesterol	73mg

1 Make the marinade. Combine the sunflower oil, clear honey, mustard, coriander seeds and orange rind and juice in a shallow dish. Mix well to combine. Crush the cardamom pods, extract the seeds and stir them into the mixture.

2 Add the prepared chicken cubes to the dish, and turn to coat them all over in the marinade. Then cover the dish and leave to marinate in the fridge for at least 2 hours.

3 Just before cooking, preheat the grill. Core the pineapple and cut it into neat wedges, leaving the skin on, if you like. Peel and slice the bananas.

4 Add the pineapple wedges and banana slices to the marinade, coating them thoroughly.

5 Drain the chicken, pineapple and banana, reserving the marinade. Thread alternately on to eight skewers. Grill on a rack under a moderate heat, turning the skewers occasionally and brushing them with the reserved marinade, for about 15 minutes until the chicken is golden and cooked through. Garnish with fresh orange segments and bay leaves.

Sweet and Sour Fish

White fish is high in protein, vitamins and minerals, but low in fat. Serve this tasty, nutritious dish with brown rice and stir-fried cabbage or spinach for a delicious lunch-time meal.

INGREDIENTS

Serves 4

60ml/4 tbsp cider vinegar
45ml/3 tbsp light soy sauce
50g/2oz/¼ cup granulated sugar
15ml/1 tbsp tomato purée
25ml/1½ tbsp cornflour
250ml/8fl oz/1 cup water
1 green pepper, seeded and sliced
225g/8oz can pineapple pieces in fruit juice
225g/8oz tomatoes, peeled and chopped
225g/8oz/2 cups button mushrooms, sliced
675g/1½lb chunky haddock fillets, skinned
salt and ground black pepper

1 Preheat the oven to 180°C/350°F/Gas 4. Mix the vinegar, soy sauce, sugar and tomato purée in a saucepan. Put the cornflour in a jug, stir in the water, then add the mixture to the saucepan, stirring well. Bring to the boil, stirring constantly until thickened. Lower the heat and simmer the sauce for 5 minutes.

2 Add the green pepper, canned pineapple pieces (with juice), tomatoes and mushrooms to the sauce and heat through. Season to taste with salt and pepper.

3 Place the fish in a single layer in a shallow ovenproof dish, pour over the sauce and cover with foil. Bake for 15–20 minutes until the fish is tender. Serve immediately.

NUTRITIONAL NOTES
Per Portion

Energy	255Kcals/1070KJ
Fat	2g
Saturated Fat	0.5g
Cholesterol	61mg

Tuna and Mixed Vegetable Pasta

INGREDIENTS

Serves 4

30ml/2 tbsp olive oil
175g/6oz/1½ cups button mushrooms, sliced
1 garlic clove, crushed
½ red pepper, seeded and chopped
15ml/1 tbsp tomato purée
300ml/½ pint/1¼ cups tomato juice
115g/4oz frozen peas
15–30ml/1–2 tbsp drained pickled green peppercorns, crushed
275g/10oz/2½ cups wholewheat pasta shapes
200g/7oz can tuna chunks in brine, drained
6 spring onions, diagonally sliced

1 Heat the oil in a pan and gently sauté the mushrooms, garlic and pepper until softened. Stir in the tomato purée, then add the tomato juice, peas and some or all of the crushed peppercorns, depending on how spicy you like the sauce. Bring to the boil, lower the heat and simmer.

2 Bring a large saucepan of lightly salted water to the boil and cook the pasta for about 12 minutes (or according to the instructions on the packet) until just tender. When the pasta is almost ready, add the tuna to the sauce and heat through gently. Stir in the spring onions. Drain the pasta, tip it into a heated bowl, and pour over the sauce. Toss to mix. Serve at once.

NUTRITIONAL NOTES
Per Portion

Energy	360Kcals/1500KJ
Fat	8g
Saturated Fat	1.5g
Cholesterol	19.5mg

Baked Stuffed Sardines

Oily fish are a good source of vitamins A and D. Serve this nutritious dish with a fresh tomato salad and fresh bread.

INGREDIENTS

Serves 4

12 fresh sardines, scaled and heads removed
15ml/1 tbsp sunflower oil, plus extra for greasing
1 onion, finely chopped
1 garlic clove, crushed
75g/3oz/1½ cups fresh wholemeal breadcrumbs
15ml/1 tbsp wholegrain mustard
30ml/2 tbsp chopped fresh parsley
1 egg yolk
30ml/2 tbsp grated Parmesan cheese
grated rind and juice of 2 lemons
salt and ground black pepper
lemon and parsley, to garnish

1 Preheat the oven to 190°C/375°F/ Gas 5. Using a sharp knife, slit the sardines open along their underside, then turn each fish over and press them firmly along the back to loosen the backbone. Remove the backbones and clean and dry the inside of each sardine thoroughly.

2 Heat the oil in a saucepan and sauté the onion and garlic gently until softened and beginning to brown.

3 Remove the pan from the heat and mix in the breadcrumbs, mustard, chopped parsley, egg yolk and Parmesan. Stir in half the lemon rind and juice and season to taste.

4 Use the stuffing to fill the cavities of the sardines.

5 Brush a shallow ovenproof dish lightly with oil and add the sardines, in a single layer. Pour over the remaining lemon rind and juice, cover with foil and bake for 30 minutes. Garnish with the lemon wedges and fresh parsley sprigs.

COOK'S TIP

Many of the larger supermarkets have fresh wet fish counters where the trained staff will happily bone your fish for you. Larger oily fish, such as mackerel or herring, could be substituted for sardines. Allow one per person.

NUTRITIONAL NOTES

Per Portion

Energy	420Kcals/1755KJ
Fat	19g
Saturated Fat	5g
Cholesterol	295mg

Monkfish with Asparagus and Pears

Monkfish is a superb firm-fleshed fish with a flavour that's often likened to lobster meat. Serve with new potatoes and broccoli.

INGREDIENTS

Serves 4

15ml/1 tbsp sunflower oil
knob of butter, for flavouring (optional)
1 medium onion, sliced
1 garlic clove, crushed
2 courgettes, diagonally sliced
2 firm dessert pears, cored and sliced
675g/1½lb monkfish tail, skinned, boned and cut into chunks
175ml/6fl oz/¾ cup medium-dry white wine or cider
175ml/6fl oz/¾ cup fish stock
225g/8oz asparagus spears, trimmed
strip of pared lemon rind
few fresh dill sprigs
45ml/3 tbsp soured cream or half-fat crème fraîche
10ml/2 tsp cornflour
salt and ground black pepper
dill sprigs, to garnish

1 Heat the oil (and butter if using) in a large frying pan. Cook the onion, garlic, courgettes and pears over a gentle heat for about 5 minutes until the onion is just beginning to brown. Using a slotted spoon, transfer the mixture to a plate.

2 Add the monkfish chunks to the fat remaining in the pan and cook for 2–3 minutes, turning frequently, until lightly browned on both sides.

3 Pour in the wine or cider and fish stock and return the vegetables and fruit to the pan.

4 Add the asparagus and lemon rind. Season with salt and pepper. Bring to the boil, then lower the heat, cover the pan and simmer gently for about 8 minutes.

5 Add the dill, replace the lid and simmer for 4–7 minutes more, until both the fish and the asparagus are tender. Discard the dill and, using a slotted spoon, remove the fish, fruit and vegetables to a warmed serving dish and keep hot.

6 Mix the soured cream or crème fraîche with the cornflour in a small bowl, then stir the mixture into the juices remaining in the pan. Cook over a gentle heat, stirring constantly, until thickened. Then pour the sauce over the fish and garnish the dish with the dill sprigs.

NUTRITIONAL NOTES
Per Portion

Energy	290Kcals/1210KJ
Fat	10.5g
Saturated Fat	4g
Cholesterol	55mg

Ginger and Lime Prawns

INGREDIENTS

Serves 4
225g/8oz peeled raw tiger prawns
⅓ cucumber
15ml/1 tbsp sunflower oil
15ml/1 tbsp sesame seed oil
175g/6oz mange-touts, trimmed
4 spring onions, diagonally sliced
30ml/2 tbsp chopped fresh coriander, to garnish

For the marinade
15ml/1 tbsp clear honey
15ml/1 tbsp light soy sauce
15ml/1 tbsp dry sherry
2 garlic cloves, crushed
small piece of fresh root ginger, peeled and finely chopped
juice of 1 lime

1 Mix together the marinade ingredients, add the prawns and leave to marinate for 1–2 hours.

2 Prepare the cucumber. Slice it in half lengthways, scoop out the seeds, then slice each half neatly into crescents. Set aside.

3 Heat both oils in a large heavy-based frying pan or wok. Drain the prawns (reserving the marinade) and stir-fry over a high heat for 4 minutes until they begin to turn pink. Add the mange-touts and the cucumber and stir-fry for 2 minutes more.

4 Stir in the reserved marinade, heat through, then stir in the spring onions and sprinkle with fresh coriander.

NUTRITIONAL NOTES
Per Portion

Energy	140Kcals/590KJ
Fat	6.5g
Saturated Fat	1g
Cholesterol	85mg

Mediterranean Fish Cutlets

INGREDIENTS

Serves 4
4 white fish cutlets, about 150g/5oz each
about 150ml/¼ pint/⅔ cup fish stock and/or dry white wine, for poaching
1 bay leaf, a few black peppercorns, and a strip of pared lemon rind, for flavouring
chopped fresh parsley, to garnish

For the tomato sauce
400g/14oz can chopped tomatoes
1 garlic clove, crushed
15ml/1 tbsp sun-dried tomato paste
15ml/1 tbsp pastis or other aniseed-flavoured liqueur
15ml/1 tbsp drained capers
12–16 stoned black olives
salt and ground black pepper

1 Heat together all the tomato sauce ingredients in a pan.

NUTRITIONAL NOTES
Per Portion

Energy	165Kcals/685KJ
Fat	3.5g
Saturated Fat	0.5g
Cholesterol	69mg

2 Place the fish in a frying pan, pour over the stock and/or wine and add the flavourings. Cover and simmer for 10 minutes or until it flakes easily.

3 Using a slotted spoon, transfer the fish to a heated dish. Strain the stock into the tomato sauce and boil to reduce slightly. Season the sauce, pour it over the fish and serve immediately, sprinkled with chopped parsley.

Middle Eastern Rice with Lentils

INGREDIENTS

Serves 4

30ml/2 tbsp sunflower oil
1 large onion, sliced
4–5 cardamom pods
2.5ml/½ tsp coriander seeds, crushed
2.5ml/½ tsp cumin seeds, crushed
small piece of fresh root ginger, peeled and finely chopped
1 cinnamon stick
1 garlic clove, crushed
115g/4oz/⅔ cup brown rice
900ml/1½ pints/3¾ cups vegetable stock
2.5ml/½ tsp ground turmeric
115g/4oz/⅔ cup split red lentils
25g/1oz/¼ cup flaked almonds, toasted
50g/2oz/⅓ cup raisins
low-fat natural yogurt, to serve

1 Heat the oil in a large saucepan and cook the onion over a gentle heat until softened. Crush the cardamom pods, extract the seeds and add them to the pan with the coriander seeds, cumin seeds, ginger, cinnamon stick and garlic. Stir over a moderate heat for 2–3 minutes.

2 Add the rice, stirring to coat the grains in the spice mixture, then pour in the stock. Stir in the turmeric. Bring to the boil, then lower the heat, cover the pan with a tight-fitting lid and simmer for 15 minutes.

3 Add the lentils to the pan, replace the lid and cook for 20 minutes more, or until the rice and lentils are tender and all the stock has been absorbed (stir in a little more stock if necessary).

4 When all the stock has been absorbed, tip the rice mixture into a heated serving dish and scatter the toasted almonds and raisins over the top. Serve with low-fat natural yogurt, if liked.

NUTRITIONAL NOTES
Per Portion

Energy	350Kcals/1465KJ
Fat	11g
Saturated Fat	1.5g
Cholesterol	0

Tagliatelle with Tomato and Courgette Sauce

INGREDIENTS

Serves 3–4
5–6 ripe tomatoes
225g/8oz wholewheat tagliatelle
30ml/2 tbsp olive oil
1 onion, chopped
2 celery sticks, chopped
1 garlic clove, crushed
2 courgettes, sliced
30ml/2 tbsp sun-dried tomato paste
50g/2oz/½ cup flaked almonds, toasted
salt and ground black pepper

1 Place the tomatoes in a bowl of boiling water for 30 seconds to loosen the skins. Peel, then chop.

2 Bring a large saucepan of lightly salted water to the boil, add the pasta and cook for about 12 minutes (or according to the instructions on the packet) until just tender.

3 Meanwhile, heat the oil in another pan and add the chopped onion, celery, garlic and courgettes. Sauté over a gentle heat for 3–4 minutes, or until the onions are softened and become lightly browned.

4 Stir in the tomatoes and sun-dried tomato paste. Cook gently for 5 minutes more, then add salt and pepper to taste.

5 Drain the pasta, return it to the pan and add the sauce. Toss well. Place in a serving dish and scatter the toasted almonds over the top to serve.

COOK'S TIP

If using fresh pasta, you'll need double the quantity, i.e. 450g/1lb for 3–4 hearty appetites. Fresh tagliatelle usually only takes 3–4 minutes to cook and is ready when it's tender but still *al dente*.

NUTRITIONAL NOTES

Per Portion (if serving 3)

Energy	495Kcals/2100KJ
Fat	22g
Saturated Fat	2.5g
Cholesterol	0

Chow Mein with Cashew Nuts

INGREDIENTS

Serves 4
30ml/2 tbsp stir-fry oil
50g/2oz/½ cup cashew nuts
2 carrots, cut into julienne sticks
3 celery sticks, cut into julienne sticks
1 green pepper, seeded and cut into thin strips
225g/8oz beansprouts
225g/8oz Chinese dried egg noodles
30ml/2 tbsp toasted sesame seeds, to garnish

For the lemon sauce
30ml/2 tbsp light soy sauce
15ml/1 tbsp dry sherry
150ml/¼ pint/⅔ cup vegetable stock
2 lemons
15ml/1 tbsp granulated sugar
10ml/2 tsp cornflour

1 Stir all the ingredients for the lemon sauce together in a jug. Bring a large saucepan of lightly salted water to the boil.

2 Heat the oil in a wok or large heavy-based frying pan. Add the cashew nuts, toss quickly over a high heat until golden, then remove with a slotted spoon.

3 Add the carrots and celery to the pan and stir-fry for 4–5 minutes. Add the pepper and beansprouts and stir-fry for 2–3 minutes more.

4 At the same time, cook the noodles in the pan of boiling water for 3 minutes (or according to the instructions on the packet).

5 Remove the vegetables from the pan with a slotted spoon. Pour in the sauce and cook for 2 minutes, stirring until thick. Return the vegetables to the pan, add the cashew nuts and stir quickly to coat in sauce.

6 Drain the noodles when cooked, tip them into a serving dish and spoon the vegetables and sauce over. Scatter with sesame seeds and serve.

NUTRITIONAL NOTES
Per Portion

Energy	460 Kcals/1925KJ
Fat	21.5g
Saturated Fat	2.5g
Cholesterol	25mg

Mushroom and Mixed Nut Roast

INGREDIENTS

Serves 4

45ml/3 tbsp sunflower seeds
45ml/3 tbsp sesame seeds
30ml/2 tbsp sunflower oil, plus extra for greasing
1 onion, roughly chopped
2 celery sticks, roughly chopped
1 green pepper, seeded and chopped
225g/8oz/2 cups mixed mushrooms, chopped
1 garlic clove, crushed
115g/4oz/2 cups fresh wholemeal breadcrumbs
115g/4oz/1 cup chopped mixed nuts
50g/2oz/⅓ cup sultanas
small piece of fresh root ginger, peeled and finely chopped
10ml/2 tsp coriander seeds, crushed
30ml/2 tbsp light soy sauce
1 egg, beaten
salt and ground black pepper
celery and coriander leaves, to garnish

For the tomato sauce

400g/14oz can chopped tomatoes
3 spring onions, chopped
30ml/2 tbsp chopped fresh coriander

NUTRITIONAL NOTES
Per Portion

Energy	460Kcals/1925KJ
Fat	37.5g
Saturated Fat	4.5g
Cholesterol	53mg

1 Grease and line a 675g/1½lb loaf tin. Sprinkle the sunflower and sesame seeds on the base.

2 Preheat the oven to 190°C/375°F/ Gas 5. Heat the oil in a frying pan, add the onion, celery, pepper, mushrooms and garlic and cook over a gentle heat for about 5 minutes until the onion has softened.

3 Mix the breadcrumbs and nuts in a large bowl. Tip in the contents of the frying pan, then stir in the sultanas, ginger, coriander seeds and soy sauce. Bind with the egg, then season.

4 Press the mixture evenly into the tin and bake for 45 minutes. Make the sauce. Heat the tomatoes in a small saucepan, add the spring onions and fresh coriander and season to taste.

5 When the loaf is cooked, loosen it with a knife, then allow to cool for a few minutes. Turn out on to a serving dish and garnish with the celery and coriander leaves. Serve with the warm tomato sauce.

Spicy Bean Hotpot

INGREDIENTS

Serves 4
225g/8oz/2 cups mushrooms
15ml/1 tbsp sunflower oil
2 onions, sliced
1 garlic clove, crushed
15ml/1 tbsp red wine vinegar
400g/14oz can chopped tomatoes
15ml/1 tbsp tomato purée
15ml/1 tbsp Worcestershire sauce or brown sauce
15ml/1 tbsp wholegrain mustard
15ml/1 tbsp soft dark brown sugar
250ml/8fl oz/1 cup vegetable stock
400g/14oz can red kidney beans, drained
400g/14oz can haricot or cannellini beans, drained
1 bay leaf
75g/3oz/½ cup raisins
salt and ground black pepper
chopped fresh parsley, to garnish

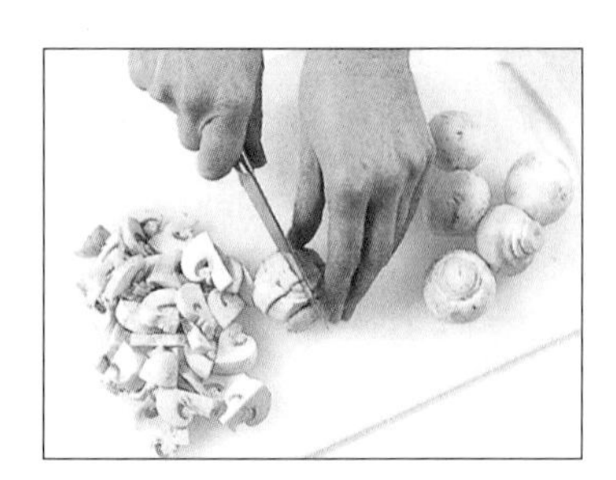

1 Wipe the mushrooms, then use a sharp vegetable knife to cut them into small pieces and set aside.

2 Heat the oil in a large saucepan or flameproof casserole, add the onions and garlic and cook over a gentle heat for 10 minutes until soft.

3 Add all the remaining ingredients except the mushrooms and seasoning. Bring to the boil, lower the heat, and simmer for 10 minutes.

4 Add the mushrooms and simmer for 5 minutes more. Stir in salt and pepper to taste. Transfer to a heated serving dish and sprinkle with parsley.

NUTRITIONAL NOTES
Per Portion

Energy	280Kcals/1175KJ
Fat	4.5g
Saturated Fat	0.5g
Cholesterol	0

Chick-pea and Spinach Curry

Chick-peas provide protein, minerals and B-group vitamins to this tasty low-fat, high-fibre curry, while spinach is a valuable vegetable source of iron. Serve this curry with brown rice or naan bread and a yogurt raita or chutney, if you like.

INGREDIENTS

Serves 3–4

30ml/2 tbsp sunflower oil
1 large onion, finely chopped
2 garlic cloves, crushed
2.5cm/1in piece of root ginger, peeled and finely chopped
1 green chilli, seeded and finely chopped
30ml/2 tbsp medium curry paste
10ml/2 tsp ground cumin
5ml/1 tsp ground turmeric
225g/8oz can chopped tomatoes
1 green or red pepper, seeded and chopped
300ml/½ pint/1¼ cups vegetable stock
15ml/1 tbsp tomato purée
450g/1lb fresh spinach
425g/15oz can chick-peas, drained
45ml/3 tbsp chopped fresh coriander
salt
5ml/1 tsp garam masala (optional)

1 Heat the sunflower oil in a large saucepan or flameproof casserole. Then add the chopped onion, crushed garlic, fresh ginger and green chilli. Cook over a gentle heat for about 5 minutes, or until the onions are softened but not browned.

2 Stir in the curry paste, cook for 1 minute more, then stir in the cumin and turmeric. Continue stirring over a low heat for 1 minute more.

3 Add the tomatoes and pepper to the pan and stir to coat with the spice mixture. Pour in the stock and stir in the tomato purée. Bring to the boil, lower the heat, cover and simmer for 15 minutes.

4 Remove any coarse stalks from the spinach, chop the leaves roughly and add them to the pan. You will probably have to do this in batches, as fresh spinach leaves are rather bulky. They cook down after about 1 minute, so this will not take very long.

5 Add the chick-peas, cover and cook gently for 5 minutes more. Stir in the fresh coriander, season with salt and sprinkle with garam masala, if using. Serve at once.

NUTRITIONAL NOTES

Per Portion

Energy	315Kcals/1310KJ
Fat	15g
Saturated Fat	1.5g
Cholesterol	0

DESSERTS AND BAKES

This is where, so often, good intentions give way to weakness and temptation. Most sweets and creamy desserts are loaded with fat and sugar and are low on nutritional value – they won't help you on the road to fitness and vitality. However, there's still a place for sweet treats made with wholegrain cereals, fruits, nuts and low-fat substitutes for the richer dairy products. This mouth-watering selection shows how easily sweet recipes may be adapted to healthier versions.

Autumn Pudding

Summer pudding is far too good to be reserved for the soft fruit season. Here is an autumn version, with apples, plums and blackberries, which makes a high-fibre dessert full of vitamins.

INGREDIENTS

Serves 6

450g/1lb eating apples
450g/1lb plums, halved and stoned
225g/8oz blackberries, hulled
60ml/4 tbsp apple juice
sugar or honey, to sweeten (optional)
8 slices of wholemeal bread, crusts removed
mint sprig and blackberry, to decorate
half-fat crème fraîche, to serve

1 Quarter the apples, remove the cores and peel, then slice them into a saucepan. Add the plums, blackberries and apple juice. Cover and cook gently for 10–15 minutes until tender. Sweeten, if necessary, with a little sugar or honey, although the fruit should be sweet enough.

2 Line the bottom and sides of a 1.2 litre/2 pint/5 cup pudding basin with 6–7 slices of bread, cut to fit. Press together tightly.

3 Spoon the fruit into the basin. Pour in just enough juice to moisten. Reserve any remaining juice.

4 Cover the fruit completely with the remaining bread. Fit a plate on top, so that it rests on the bread just below the rim. Stand the basin in a larger bowl to catch any juice. Place a weight on the plate and chill overnight.

5 Turn the pudding out on to a plate and pour the reserved juice over any areas which have not absorbed the juice. Decorate with the mint sprig and blackberry and serve with crème fraîche.

NUTRITIONAL NOTES

Per Portion

Energy	185Kcals/765KJ
Fat	1.5g
Saturated Fat	0.5g
Cholesterol	0

Fragrant Rice with Mango Purée

Nuts, dried fruit, cardamom and rosewater make this Indian-style rice pudding a real treat.

INGREDIENTS

Serves 6

2 ripe mangoes
50g/2oz/⅓ cup basmati rice
1.5 litres/2½ pints/6 cups semi-skimmed milk
50g/2oz/⅓ cup demerara sugar
50g/2oz/⅓ cup sultanas
5ml/1 tsp rosewater
5 cardamom pods
45ml/3 tbsp orange juice
20g/¾oz/scant ¼ cup flaked almonds, toasted
20g/¾oz/scant ¼ cup pistachio nuts, chopped

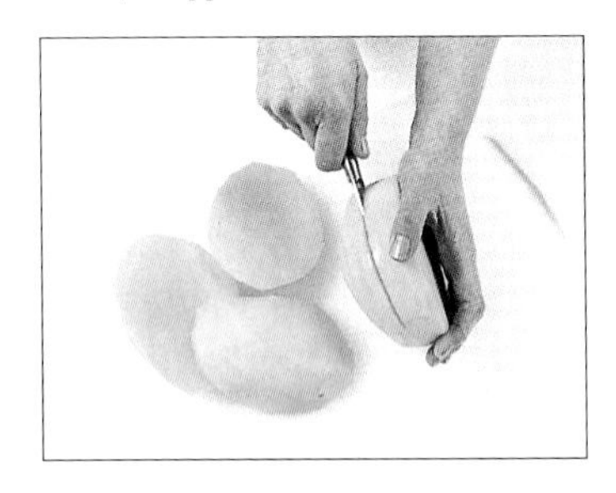

1 Using a sharp knife, peel, slice and stone the mangoes.

2 Preheat the oven to 150°C/300°F/Gas 2. Put the basmati rice in an ovenproof dish. Boil the milk then pour it over the rice. Bake uncovered for 2 hours until the rice has become soft and mushy.

3 Remove the dish from the oven and stir in the demerara sugar and sultanas, with half the rosewater. Crush the cardamom pods, extract the seeds and stir them into the rice mixture. Allow to cool.

4 Place the mango flesh in a blender or food processor. Add the orange juice and remaining rosewater. Blend until smooth.

5 Divide the mango purée among six individual glass serving dishes. Spoon the rice pudding mixture evenly over the top. Leave to chill thoroughly in the fridge or a cool place.

6 When ready to serve, scatter the toasted almonds and chopped pistachio nuts over the top of each pudding.

NUTRITIONAL NOTES

Per Portion

Energy	300Kcals/1260KJ
Fat	8g
Saturated Fat	3g
Cholesterol	17.5mg

Fruit Fondue with Hazelnut Dip

Ingredients

Serves 2

selection of fresh fruits for dipping, such as satsumas, kiwi fruit, grapes, physalis and whole strawberries
50g/2oz/½ cup reduced-fat soft cheese
150ml/5fl oz/⅔ cup low-fat hazelnut yogurt
5ml/1 tsp vanilla essence
5ml/1 tsp caster sugar

Nutritional Notes
Per Portion (Dip only)

Energy	170Kcals/714KJ
Fat	4g
Saturated Fat	2.5g
Cholesterol	6.5mg

1 First prepare the fruits. Peel and segment the satsumas. Then peel the kiwi fruit and cut into wedges. Wash the grapes and peel back the papery casing on the physalis.

2 Beat the soft cheese with the yogurt, vanilla essence and sugar in a bowl. Stir in three-quarters of the hazelnuts. Spoon into a glass serving dish set on a platter or small pots on individual plates and scatter over the remaining hazelnuts. Arrange the prepared fruits around the dip and serve immediately.

Yogurt Sundaes with Passion Fruit Coulis

Here is a sundae you can enjoy every day! The frozen yogurt has less fat and fewer calories than traditional ice cream and the fruits provide vitamins A and C.

Ingredients

Serves 4

350g/12oz strawberries, hulled and halved
2 passion fruits, halved
10ml/2 tsp icing sugar (optional)
2 ripe peaches, stoned and chopped
8 scoops (about 350g/12oz) vanilla or strawberry frozen yogurt

Nutritional Notes
Per Portion

Energy	135Kcals/560KJ
Fat	1g
Saturated Fat	0.5g
Cholesterol	3.5mg

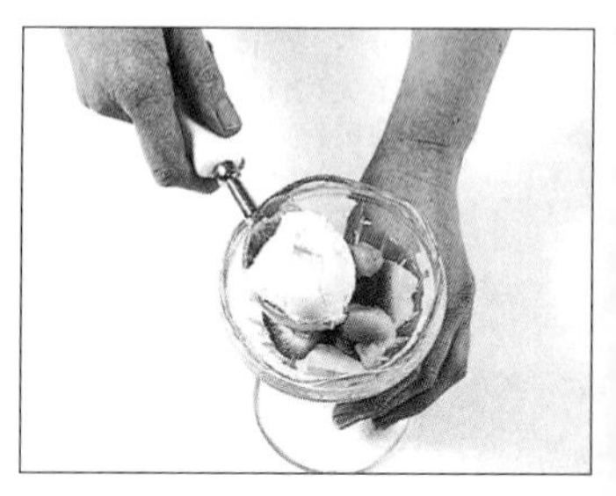

1 Purée half the strawberries. Scoop out the passion fruit pulp and add it to the coulis. Sweeten, if necessary.

2 Spoon half the remaining strawberries and half the chopped peaches into four tall sundae glasses. Top each dessert with a scoop of frozen yogurt. Set aside a few choice pieces of fruit for decoration, and use the rest to make a further layer on the top of each sundae. Top each with a final scoop of frozen yogurt.

3 Pour over the passion fruit coulis and decorate the sundaes with the reserved strawberries and pieces of peach. Serve immediately.

Apple and Blackcurrant Pancakes

These pancakes are made with a wholewheat batter and are filled with a delicious fruit mixture.

Ingredients

Makes 8

115g/4oz/1 cup plain wholemeal flour
300ml/½ pint/1¼ cups skimmed milk
1 egg, beaten
15ml/1 tbsp sunflower oil, plus extra for greasing
half-fat crème fraîche, to serve (optional)
toasted nuts or sesame seeds, for sprinkling (optional)

For the filling

450g/1lb cooking apples
225g/8oz blackcurrants
30–45ml/2–3 tbsp water
30ml/2 tbsp demerara sugar

1 Make the pancake batter. Place the flour in a mixing bowl and make a well in the centre.

2 Add a little of the milk with the egg and the oil. Whisk the flour into the liquid then gradually whisk in the rest of the milk, keeping the batter smooth and free from lumps. Cover the batter and chill while you prepare the filling.

3 Quarter, peel and core the apples. Slice them into a pan and add the blackcurrants and water. Cook over a gentle heat for 10–15 minutes until the fruit is soft. Stir in enough demerara sugar to sweeten.

4 Lightly grease a pancake pan with just a smear of oil. Heat the pan, pour in about 30ml/2 tbsp batter, swirl it around and cook for about 1 minute. Flip the pancake over with a palette knife and cook the other side. Keep hot while cooking the remaining pancakes (unless cooking to order).

5 Fill the pancakes with the apple and blackcurrant mixture and roll them up. Serve with a dollop of crème fraîche, if using, and sprinkle with nuts or sesame seeds, if liked.

Nutritional Notes

Per Portion

Energy	120Kcals/505KJ
Fat	3g
Saturated Fat	0.5g
Cholesterol	25mg

Warm Bagels with Poached Apricots

Ingredients

Serves 4

a few strips of orange peel
225g/8oz/1⅓ cups ready-to-eat dried apricots
250ml/8fl oz/1 cup fresh orange juice
2.5ml/½ tsp orange flower water
2 cinnamon and raisin bagels
20ml/4 tsp reduced-sugar orange marmalade
60ml/4 tbsp half-fat crème fraîche or soured cream
15g/½ oz/2 tbsp chopped pistachio nuts, to decorate

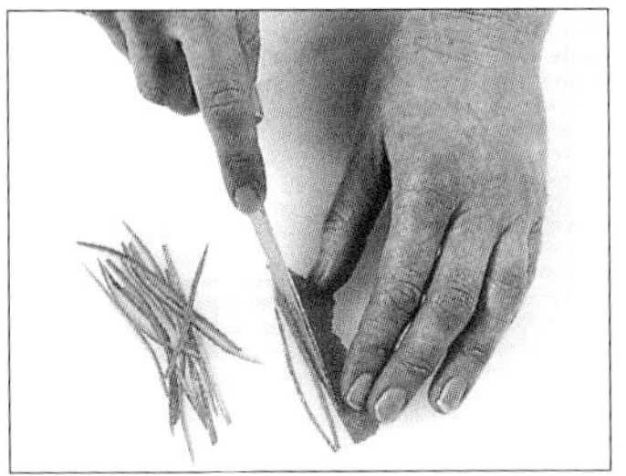

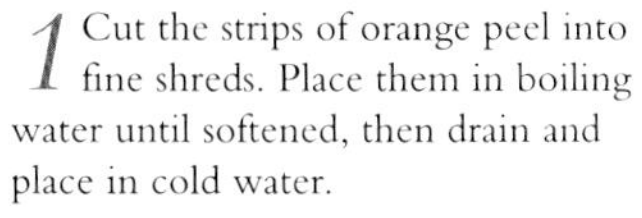

1 Cut the strips of orange peel into fine shreds. Place them in boiling water until softened, then drain and place in cold water.

2 Preheat the oven to 160°C/325°F/Gas 3. Combine the apricots and orange juice in a small saucepan. Heat gently for about 10 minutes until the juice has reduced and looks syrupy. Allow to cool, then stir in the orange flower water. Meanwhile, place the bagels on a baking sheet and warm in the oven for 5–10 minutes.

3 Split the bagels in half horizontally. Lay one half, crumb uppermost, on each serving plate. Spread 5ml/1 tsp orange marmalade on each bagel.

4 Spoon 15ml/1 tbsp crème fraîche or soured cream into the centre of each bagel and place a quarter of the apricot compôte at the side. Scatter orange peel and pistachio nuts over the top to decorate. Serve immediately.

Nutritional Notes

Per Portion

Energy	260Kcals/1090KJ
Fat	9g
Saturated Fat	4g
Cholesterol	51.5mg

Cranberry Oat Flapjack

Here's a real tea-time treat for everybody to enjoy!

INGREDIENTS

Makes 14
150g/5oz/1½ cups porridge oats
115g/4oz/⅔ cup demerara sugar
75g/3oz/½ cup dried cranberries
115g/4oz/½ cup polyunsaturated margarine, melted
oil, for greasing

COOK'S TIP

Dried cranberries are a relatively new product, available from larger supermarkets. They have a sweet yet slightly tart flavour and their bright red colour will add visual appeal. They can be used to replace more usual dried fruits, such as sultanas.

1 Preheat the oven to 190°C/375°F/ Gas 5. Grease a shallow 28 x 18cm/ 11 x 7in tin.

2 Stir the oats, sugar and cranberries together in a bowl. Pour in the melted margarine and stir thoroughly until combined.

NUTRITIONAL NOTES
Per Flapjack

Energy	150Kcals/635KJ
Fat	8g
Saturated Fat	1.5g
Cholesterol	0.5mg

3 Press the oat and cranberry mixture into the prepared tin. Bake for 15–20 minutes, until golden.

4 Remove the flapjack from the oven and mark into 14 bars, then leave to cool for 5 minutes, in the tin. Remove the bars and place on a wire rack to cool completely. Store for up to 5 days in an airtight container.

Rhubarb and Raspberry Cranachan

INGREDIENTS

Serves 4
350g/12oz rhubarb
30ml/2 tbsp unsweetened orange juice
175g/6oz raspberries
30ml/2 tbsp pure fruit raspberry jam
25g/1oz/⅓ cup porridge oats
25g/1oz/¼ cup mixed chopped nuts
200ml/7fl oz/scant 1 cup light vanilla yogurt

NUTRITIONAL NOTES
Per Portion

Energy	135Kcals/565KJ
Fat	5.5g
Saturated Fat	1g
Cholesterol	2mg

1 Cut the rhubarb into chunks. Heat the orange juice in a saucepan and poach the rhubarb gently for 8–10 minutes until just tender. Remove from the heat immediately. Allow to cool, then stir in the raspberries and pure fruit jam.

2 Spread the oats and nuts out on a baking sheet and toast them briefly under a hot grill.

3 Spoon the fruit mixture into four sundae dishes. Top each portion with yogurt, then scatter the toasted oats and nuts over the top.

Wholemeal Apple, Apricot and Walnut Loaf

INGREDIENTS

Makes 10–12 slices

225g/8oz/2 cups plain wholemeal flour
5ml/1 tsp baking powder
pinch of salt
115g/4oz/½ cup sunflower margarine
175g/6oz/1 cup soft light brown sugar
2 size 2 eggs, lightly beaten
grated rind and juice of 1 orange
50g/2oz/½ cup chopped walnuts
50g/2oz/⅓ cup ready-to-eat dried apricots, chopped
1 large cooking apple
oil, for greasing

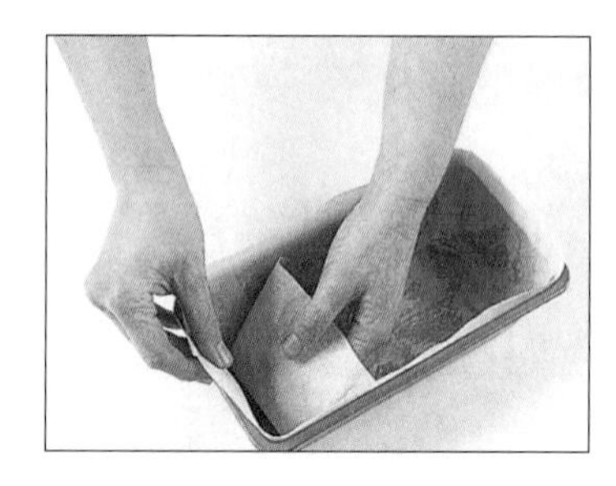

1 Preheat the oven to 180°C/350°F/Gas 4. Line and grease a 900g/2lb loaf tin.

2 Sift the flour, baking powder and salt into a large mixing bowl, then tip the bran remaining in the sieve into the mixture. Add the margarine, sugar, eggs, orange rind and juice. Stir, then beat with a hand-held electric beater until smooth.

3 Stir in the walnuts and apricots. Quarter, peel and core the apple, chop it roughly and add it to the mixture. Stir, then spoon the mixture into the prepared tin and level the top.

4 Bake for 1 hour, or until a skewer inserted into the centre of the loaf comes out clean. Cool in the tin for about 5 minutes, then turn the loaf out on to a wire rack and peel off the lining paper. When cold, store in an airtight tin.

NUTRITIONAL NOTES

Per Slice (if cutting into 10)

Energy	290Kcals/1220KJ
Fat	14.5g
Saturated Fat	2.5g
Cholesterol	43.5mg

Spiced Banana Muffins

Wholemeal muffins, with banana for added fibre, make a delicious treat at any time of the day. If liked, slice off the tops and fill with a teaspoon of reduced-sugar jam or marmalade.

INGREDIENTS

Makes 12

75g/3oz/$^{3}/_{4}$ cup plain wholemeal flour
50g/2oz/$^{1}/_{2}$ cup plain white flour
10ml/2 tsp baking powder
pinch of salt
5ml/1 tsp mixed spice
40g/1$^{1}/_{2}$oz/$^{1}/_{4}$ cup soft light brown sugar
50g/2oz/$^{1}/_{4}$ cup polyunsaturated margarine
1 egg, beaten
150ml/$^{1}/_{4}$ pint/$^{2}/_{3}$ cup semi-skimmed milk
grated rind of 1 orange
1 ripe banana
20g/$^{3}/_{4}$oz/$^{1}/_{4}$ cup porridge oats
20g/$^{3}/_{4}$oz/scant $^{1}/_{4}$ cup chopped hazelnuts

1 Preheat the oven to 200°C/400°F/ Gas 6. Line a muffin tin with 12 large paper cake cases. Sift together both flours, the baking powder, salt and mixed spice into a bowl, then tip the bran remaining in the sieve into the bowl. Stir in the sugar.

2 Melt the margarine and pour it into a mixing bowl. Cool slightly, then beat in the egg, milk and grated orange rind.

3 Gently fold in the dry ingredients. Mash the banana with a fork, then stir it gently into the mixture, being careful not to overmix.

NUTRITIONAL NOTES *Per Muffin*	
Energy	110Kcals/465KJ
Fat	5g
Saturated Fat	1g
Cholesterol	17.5mg

4 Spoon the mixture into the paper cases. Combine the oats and hazelnuts and sprinkle a little of the mixture over each muffin.

5 Bake for 20 minutes until the muffins are well risen and golden, and a skewer inserted in the centre comes out clean. Transfer to a wire rack and serve warm or cold.

Index